Public House and Beverage Management

Key principles and issues

Michael Flynn, Caroline Ritchie and Andrew Roberts

BUTTERWORTH
HEINEMANN

OXFORD AUCKLAND BOSTON JOHANNESBURG MELBOURNE NEW DELHI

Butterworth-Heinemann
Linacre House, Jordan Hill, Oxford OX2 8DP
225 Wildwood Avenue, Woburn, MA 01801-2041
A division of Reed Educational and Professional Publishing Ltd

   A member of the Reed Elsevier plc group

First published 2000

British Library Cataloguing in Publication Data
Flynn, Michael
   Public house and beverage management: key principles and
   issues
   1. Bars (Drinking establishments) – Management
   I. Title   II. Ritchie, Caroline   III. Roberts, Andrew
   647.9'5'068

ISBN 0 7506 4678 0

Composition by Genesis Typesetting, Rochester, Kent
Printed and bound in Great Britain

Contents

Figures and tables

Figures

Tables

Preface

In 1998 the School of Hospitality, Tourism and Leisure at the University of Wales Institute, Cardiff (UWIC) decided to expand the range of courses available. It was felt that there was a need to provide a specialist course in the area of licensed trade management, given the ever-increasing importance of this sector to the hospitality industry generally. During the process of setting up the initial HND, the authors noted that there were currently no core books suitable for such a course, and so the idea of *Public House and Beverage Management* was born. This book is intended to provide essential, basic background information to all level one and two courses which specialize in Licensed Trade, as well as useful information to all those studying Hospitality and International Hospitality courses. The book should also prove useful to those people currently working in the industry who are starting to develop a management career as a licensee.

It is hoped that eventually this book will merely be the first of a number of publications that add to the general body of knowledge in this newly developing sector of the leisure industries.

Michael Flynn, Caroline Ritchie and Andrew Roberts

Acknowledgements

The authors would like to thank individually their peers and members of their families who have suffered from the moments of deep stress the authors have gone through in order to write this book. However, as this would take another book, they would particularly like to thank Ken Tressider for his tolerance and help in proofreading almost the whole book, from its raw state to the final draft. They would also like to thank Mike Snelgrove whose frequent assistance with information technology, both specialist knowledge of industry systems and how to operate various packages, proved invaluable.

The authors also received much help from current practitioners within the industry, and would particularly like to thank Chris Parr of S. A. Brain and Company Limited, for his time and his reference book, which we will return as soon as possible. Our thanks also to all those who patiently answered our questions and so have contributed invaluable information to the general body of knowledge concerning the licensed trade industry.

A history of the licensed trade industry

In the beginning

> For ten thousand years, ever since human beings settled down to the cultivation of cereals and vines, alcohol has played a fundamental role in society. It has served as an object of religious ritual, a focus of secular ceremonies and a lubricant of social inter-course; it has been employed as an aid to the digestion of food, a means of slaking thirst without risk of contracting disease and a source of nutrition in its own right; it has been used in the treatment of wounds and disease and as both a stimulant and a sedative – as well as being valued for its taste. (Barr, 1995: 1)

There are many biblical references to social drinking as well as it being a fundamental element in many Christian sacraments, with a preference for stimulating drinks rather than water. But the very earliest brewers were elsewhere, in Egypt.

The ancient brewers

The earliest records of the brewing of ale can been seen on the frescos in the Egyptian temples.

> In Egypt, five thousand years ago, the ancient City of Pelusium was as noted for its Breweries as for its

University. A thousand years later the Egyptian reformer was demanding the reduction of the number of Alehouses then existing in the land. The outcry could have had little practical effect, as yet another thousand years later the students of the University of Pelusium were found neglecting their studies for the seduction of the beer houses. (Hackwood, 1994: 30)

Primitive man, being nomadic, would have doubtless contented himself with the fermentation of drinks made from wild honey or wild fruits. When primitive man settled, the art of brewing using corn was developed. The UK, like the Nile valley, is ill suited to the cultivation of the vine and, therefore, the national beverage of both countries became beer. It has been suggested that inns made their appearance in the UK from the earliest dawn of civilization. 'Herodotus ascribes the first discovery of the art of brewing "Barley Wine" to Isis, the wife of Osiris; and a beverage of this nature, perhaps made from wheat, barley and honey, is mentioned by Xenophon, 401 BC' (Hackwood, 1994: 30).

Some non-alcoholics

Barr writes:

> Followers of the prophet Mohammed are forbidden to drink alcohol. According to legend, the prohibition was imposed following an incident that occurred while the prophet's disciples were drinking together after a dinner in Medina. One of his Meccan followers began to recite an uncomplimentary poem about the tribe of Medina, whereupon one of his Medinite followers picked up a bone from the table and hit the Meccan on the head. Although the wound was not serious, the incident caused Mohammed such concern that he asked Allah how he could prevent it from happening again. Allah replied, 'Believers, wine and games of chance, idols of divining arrows, are abominations devised by Satan. Avoid them so that you may prosper. Satan seeks to stir up enmity and hatred among you by means of wine and gambling, and to keep you from remembrance of Allah and from your prayers'. (Barr, 1995: 1)

Several hundred years later, an alternative to alcohol was found in the form of coffee, and coffee houses were used as an alternative to taverns. They were not popular with religious zealots who felt that the Koran did not explicitly permit the innovation. In the Ottoman Empire the coffee shops were closed down after it was found that Sultan Osman II was murdered by mutinous members of the imperial guard who were inclined to frequent and scheme in coffee shops. The coffee houses were re-established until Mehmed Koprulu closed them in 1665 when many critics of the war with Venice were meeting in coffee houses. Koprulu imposed extremely stringent punishments upon those who disobeyed his order: for a first violation, the offender was to be cudgelled; for a second, he was to be sewn into a leather bag and thrown into the Bosporos; there would consequently be no likelihood of a third violation (Barr, 1995: 4)

Westernized drinking habits

The Romans

As the Egyptian empire declined, the Greeks and the Romans became more powerful, the wine of the grape became the beverage of civilization and, as the Romans constructed roads throughout their empire, there was a need to build what were called *mutationes* – places where post-horses could be taken to be watered, fed or exchanged. Also at points along the roads, wherever the volume of traffic warranted it, were hostelries for man and horse known as *Tabernae diversoriae* which were the prototype for the road-side taverns or old English wayside hostelry. Alcohol would have been available but was not an important part of their role. Roman inns were places for social gathering where chess was regularly played and the doors were often painted in chequered patterns. Chequers is still an inn sign used today.

The Anglo-Saxons

As the Roman empire declined, the influence of the Northern European invaders led to a major shift to malt liquor. Ale was considered the beverage of the gods, and drunkenness was regarded as rather honourable – the man who could withstand the strongest drink was fervently admired and well respected. The Danes were thought to have been responsible for large-scale excessive drinking and the word 'ale' came into the English language from the Danish 'ol'. The English started to drink ale as a daily beverage at this time.

The Anglo-Saxons had three types of establishments open to the public:

- the alehouse (*eala-hus*)
- the wine-house (*win-hus*)
- the inn (*cumen-hus*).

Accommodation was very hard to find on a long journey and travellers would often depend on the goodwill of local residents.

Religious houses were used to entertain travellers who would be allowed to stay up to three days upon request.

As long ago as AD 616 the laws of Ethelbert were the predecessors of our modern licensing laws. Since then there have always been restrictions on the sale and the consumption of strong drink. Ina, King of Wessex set up laws to regulate the numerous alehouses in AD 728.

Early brewing

Little is known about the Celts and brewing, although there are records of drunkenness. St Gildas wrote a poem about the 'Battle of Cattraeth' in Lothian, in which he accuses the British chieftains of going into battle drunk.

The Olde English monasteries were the centres of excellence for the art of brewing. Sir Walter Scott in his novel *Ivanhoe* mentions the reputation of the Burton upon Trent monastery for quality ale. There are records of this conventional beer in 1295 when it was sometimes known as 'Cicero', and Mary Queen of Scots was known to have been supplied with beer when imprisoned in Tutbury Castle in 1584. It should be noted that medieval England did not know about tea, coffee or spirits such as brandy, gin and rum. Wine was considered a wealthy man's beverage.

Hackworth writes:

> It appears that the great carrying business, so widely known as Pickfords, was established in 1640, when road traffic had to be performed mainly by the use of pack-horses, and has only grown to its present enormous dimensions by the overcoming of trade rivalry from time to time. In 1723 there was a small carrier near Burton. His name was Bass. Upon his round he sold a home-brewed beer prepared in his spare time. The demand for the beverage grew to such an extent that he sold his carrying business to Pickfords and devoted himself exclusively to brewing. Such was the commencement of the great Burton house of Bass. (Hackwood, 1994: 42)

Ale and beer at this time were differentiated by their quality. Beer would be sold at twice the price of ale as it was the brew from the first mashing of the malt and considered superior. It is probable that there is an association between the word 'beer' and barley. The term 'beer' was infrequently heard until it was used to distinguish ale from hopped ale. Nowadays ale is considered superior to beer, with beer embracing all malt liquors, whereas ale does not apply to stout or porter. The marking of barrels with 'X', 'XX' or 'XXX' was first used as a trademark guarantee signifying the monks had sworn on the cross that the beer was of sound quality. The three categories were Pale, Mild or Strong ales.

Medieval times

Accommodation was in limited supply and travel was increasing. The monasteries expanded their role in accommodating travellers and wayfarers. Many of these guesthouses were attached to a chapel and the guests would use it to seek the protection of the saints for the remainder of their journey. They would make offerings to the religious foundations that produced a lucrative income. Without the blessing of any truly authentic records it is difficult to be completely accurate about just how these establishments were run, but the monastic lodging houses, such as the 'Pilgrims' inn at Glastonbury, the 'Bell' at Tewkesbury and the 'New Inn' at Gloucester, were the forerunners of the inn.

The 'New Inn' still stands to this day in Gloucester, much to the delight of many modern-day tourists, and was described as follows in the *Gloucester Chronicle*:

> The assassination of Edward II, at Berkeley Castle, his burial at Gloucester, and the excitement consequent thereon in religious bodies, combined to attract large numbers of pilgrims to the shrine in the Cathedral. To accommodate these, large hostelries were built on the site of the 'Old' Inn. Rudge says that in the time of Abbot Seabrook, who presided over the monastery from 1400 to 1457, the New Inn, in Northgate Street, was built by John Twyning, a monk, who caused an underground passage to be made from it to the Abbey. The New Inn was spacious, and was constructed of ponderous materials. The buildings surrounded two square courts, and, so far as can be seen, were provided with stairs leading to two tier galleries. These led to numerous large and small rooms. It was commonly said to be built of chestnut-large beams, the spaces filled with brick nogging and plaster. (Cited in Hackwood, 1994: 228)

The term 'inn' is of Saxon origin signifying a chamber and was later used as a general term for a mansion. The *Concise English Dictionary* (1992) definition of 'inn' is 'n. A public house of lodging and entertainment for travellers; *Lodging, abode; *a place of residence or hostel for students. *v.i. To stay at the inn. *v.t. To lodge and entertain'.

The inn of these times was primarily a lodging house with little importance placed on the sale of alcohol. There are many examples of inns, which were previously the mansions of the nobility. Lincoln's Inn was originally the residence of the Earl of Lincoln and Gray's Inn the town house of the Lords Gray. The term 'inn' was originally used for the guesthouses, which housed the scholars seeking lodgings in Oxford and Cambridge before they became the halls of residence. Similarly the Inns of Court were lodgings for law students.

It is useful to look at the *Concise English Dictionary* (1992) definition of 'Hotel' and 'hostel' to clarify their role: 'Hostel n. An Inn; a house or extra-collegiate hall for the residence of students, etc.; a place of residence not run commercially' and 'Hotel A superior Inn for the entertainment of strangers and travellers; in France, a town residence or mansion'.

The mansions, which were transformed into inns, would hang their heraldic signs at the front of the buildings, a custom, which is still used to this day outside many public houses.

The customers of the inns would generally be the middle classes, the merchants, packmen and landowners. The rich would prefer the hospitality of the monasteries, as they were the founders and patrons of such establishments, and the monks, out of charity, would accommodate the very poor who could not afford the inns.

The medieval inn would have been very basic with all the beds in one large room, and the victuals would have been meat, bread and a little beer. In order to stop the innkeepers from exploiting the guests, Parliament prepared a statute to compel innkeepers to sell food at a reasonable tariff.

Travellers would also have had the opportunity of stopping at alehouses, which were lesser establishments, found more frequently, mainly at road crossings. They were instantly recognized by the 'ale stake', which was a long pole with a thick brush at the top. Their reputation was notoriously bad, with many travellers not wishing to be seen entering them.

Restrictive legislation was necessary in the Edwardian period to control the alehouses and wine taverns, which were being used merely as drinking shops. The innkeeper needed to be seen as having primarily a lodging house, and for this not to degenerate to a drinking shop. There was a clear distinction between these two categories of public house: alehouses had to be licensed. 'If any ale-house keeper or innkeeper refused to lodge a traveller, a justice of the peace might compel him to it; or the constable might present it as an offence at the next sessions; or the party refused might have an action on the case' (Hackwood, 1994: 67).

As the alehouses increased in numbers, so their reputation continued to suffer. Stow, who wrote about London between 1560 and 1590, depicted a house of ill repute as follows:

> One Wotton, a gentleman born, and sometimes a Merchant of good credit, but failing by time into decay . . . kept an ale house at Smart's – very near Billingsgate. . . . And in the same house he procured all the cutpurses about the city to repair to his house. There was a

school-house set up, to learn young boys to cut purses: two devices were hung up, the one was a pocket, the other was a purse. The pocket had in it certain counters, and it was hung about the Hawks bells, and over the top did hang a little sacring bell. The purse had silver in it. And he that could take out a counter without any noise was allowed to be a public foyster. And he that could take out a piece of silver out of the purse without noise of any of the bells was adjudged a judicial Nypper, according to their art. A Foyster was a pickpocket, a Nypper was a pickpurse or Cutpurse. (Hackwood, 1994: 69).

The seventeenth century: spirits, tea and coffee

By the end of the sixteenth century, the manufacture of spirits on the Continent now became available in the UK. British troops were introduced to the habit of drinking spirits while fighting in the Low Countries. The term 'Dutch courage' is a term still used today, which reflected from the Dutch soldier's habit of going into battle after drinking copious quantities of spirits.

The introduction of spirits, tea and coffee reduced the sales of ale, which in turn meant the consumption of home-grown barley, wheat and malt fell. The situation deteriorated when Parliament introduced excise taxes in 1643 on beer, cider and perry in order to increase revenue to aid the cost of the Civil War. The new beverages caused such concern that in 1673 a petition was presented to Parliament asking for their prohibition. Excise taxes were introduced after the reformation on spirits, tea and coffee. These taxes were very unpopular and led to a lot of discontent, although these taxes were low compared to the astronomical figures of today.

The licensed breweries saw a dramatic drop in the sale of ales, and drinking habits changed for ever. A new spirit was to become very popular with the working classes; the juniper-flavoured English gin was distilled and retailed on a large scale using home-grown corn. To spite the French, Parliament prohibited the sale of brandy, and other foreign spirits soon followed. Gin shops rapidly developed creating a new set of problems.

It was in the 1650s that coffee was introduced to Western Europe and the first coffee houses were opened in England. They were very popular with the middle classes and only temperance drinks were served. They were also considered centres for plots and counterplots, and King Charles II prepared a proclamation for the suppression of coffee shops, whereby all coffee-houses would be closed on 10 January, 1676. Public hostility was so great that on 8 January another proclamation was issued, overturning the earlier one.

1700–1800: the gin debacle

The government policy of actively encouraging the distilling of gin led to a rapid increase in retail sales.

> In 1736 the 'Drinking of Geneva,' it was alleged had become constant and excessive among the lower orders of the population, destroying thousands and rendering tens of thousands unfit to labour; it was debauching the morals of the nation and leading to an increase of crime.
>
> In London one house in every four was a gin-shop, for the spirit was retailed by tradesmen who dealt in other commodities; it was even sold from stables, sheds and wheelbarrows; gin was so cheap it was not uncommon for a sign to read 'Here a man may get drunk for a penny, and dead drunk for twopence'. (Hackworth, 1994: 128)

The government attempted to address this issue with the Gin Act of 1736, with taxes, retailers having to pay £50 for a licence to sell gin. The discontent was palpable, with mobs on the streets; a double guard was placed on Kensington Palace, and guards on horseback paraded in the Covent Garden area to quell any unrest. By 1743 the consumption of gin was still increasing, with the illicit sale of gin out of control. New legislation, directed at controlling the illicit sale of gin, reduced the retail licence duty from £50 to £1 and the excise duty was abolished. The gin problem did not improve and drunkenness, brutality and degradation increased.

The wealthy were drinking excessively, with gentlemen at social parties drinking two bottles of wine each and drunkenness considered as acceptable behaviour. The lower classes would drink beer as well as gin in large quantities on a daily basis.

Fresh efforts to control the problems were implemented in 1751, and proved to be considerably more successful than the impractical measures of the past. The significant changes were that distillers were prohibited from selling to either retail or unlicensed public houses, and that debts for drink should not be recoverable by law. Very gradually the trend moved away from gin to malt liquors.

Coffee shops were increasing in number and frequented by the middle classes. They gained the nickname of 'penny universities' because the drink cost a penny and customers spent their time discussing the issues of the day.

The 1800s

In 1830, the Beer House Act was passed, allowing any householder to obtain a licence to sell beer by retail on payment of 2 guineas. The beer could be sold for consumption on or off the premises. Some 31 000 beer licences were issued in the first year, sometimes to dwellings next to each other. The gin shops continued to flourish as they could now sell drink on or off the premises with a beer licence. The 1830s saw the first 'gin palaces'. They were places of splendour compared to the slums of the city dwellers. 'Beer and Porter are the natural beverage of the Englishman . . . the increase in Gin-drinking and that of suicides, murders, and all kinds of violence, are contemporaneous' (*The Times*, October and December 1829, cited in Hackworth, 1994).

The Industrial Revolution rapidly created huge inner city populations and in the early 1830s there was chaos on the streets with all-night drinking on Saturday nights, particularly outside the gin palaces, with people sleeping in the gutters, fighting, swearing and shouting general obscenities. This was to lead to the beginning of the restriction of opening hours. In 1839 a Metropolitan Police Act prohibited the opening of public houses in the metropolis before 1.00 p.m. on a Sunday, to encourage the men to go home. As a result, there was a 35 per cent reduction in people apprehended for drunk and disorderly conduct. Such was the success, that in 1865 the Public House Closing Acts forbade the selling of liquor between 1.00 a.m. and 4.00 p.m., except to lodgers. The Liberal government introduced a Licensing Act in 1872, which fixed the weekday closing time at midnight in London, and 11.00 p.m. elsewhere. The law was only applied to pubs used by the working classes, leading to riots in Liverpool and Coventry angered at 'one rule for the rich and another for the poor'. The Act was one of the main reasons for the Liberal defeat of 1874. Disraeli rewarded the publicans by giving them an extra half an hour opening time in London, to 12.30 a.m. Neither party chose to meddle with the opening hours again until the First World War.

The public houses in the mid–1800s were now becoming unique buildings in their own right. They found that entertainment was boosting sales. Music and song became very popular. One of the first of a new standard of public house was 'The Eagle Tavern' in Shepherdess Walk off the City Road, London, which was rebuilt in 1839–40.

The Eagle set a new standard of splendour for public houses, which was not to be equalled for many years. But then the Eagle was unlike any other pub. The original tavern, with a garden at the back, was acquired in the 1820s by Thomas Rouse. He developed it into one of the main pleasure resorts in early Victorian London. Its amenities can be gathered from an advertisement of 1838, listing the pleasure grounds, the brilliant illuminations of variegated lamps, in stars, wreaths, and mottos; the beautifully painted cosmoramas, the set scenes in the grounds. The magic mirrors, the Olympic Temple, the Saloon, the double band, the great French rope-dancers,

with the infant prodigies, the Grotesque brothers, standard and select vaudevilles, laughable ballets, and the
peculiar extravaganza, the pas de coco, together with a
first rate concert of vocal and instrumental music.
(Girouard, 1990: 35)

As the Victorian public house developed, alternative venues for
social gatherings were developing. The coffee houses, which had
always been considered the domain of the wealthy and the
middle classes, were now being adapted in the war against
alcohol by the temperance lobby. The plan was to offer the
working classes an opportunity to meet socially without the
distraction of alcohol.

Coffee public houses

These first opened in 1853 in Dundee and followed the concept of
the coffee-house design. They offered guests good value for
money food, which was lacking in public houses.

British workman's public houses

The first one opened in Leeds. Unlike the coffee public house the
British workman's public houses were dry imitations of pubs.
They spread rapidly in the North of England and reached
London in the 1870s. Dr Barnado's was responsible for the
transformation of the Edinburgh Castle pub, Limehouse, into the
Edinburgh Castle Coffee Palace, and made a similar conversion
to the Dublin Castle, Mile End Road. They were both situated in
areas of great deprivation.

Peoples Café Company

These cafés were based on the continental café. Their popularity
flourished when the subsidies from the well-intentioned sponsors expired, by offering good value food and refreshments to the
working class who found the cafés cheap and useful.

The two most successful chains of working-men's cafés
in London were Lockhart's Cocoa Rooms and Pearce
and Plenty Ltd. The latter were started in the 1880s by
John Pearce, a Temperance-pledge porter in Covent
Garden who had worked his way up to them by selling
coffee from a costermonger's barrow painted like a fire
engine and named 'The Gutter Hotel'. The Aerated
Bread Company shops, founded in about 1854, and the
Lyons tea shops, founded in 1894, were on a slightly
higher level and aimed at a clientele of clerks and
white-collar workers rather than working men. (Girouard,
1990: 206)

The Coffee Tavern Company

This rapidly expanded, the Coffee Public House Association encouraging new investment with competitive loans to those who wished to open new houses. The non-alcoholic drinks available in addition to coffee, were tea, milk, cocoa, lemonade and soda water. Non-alcoholic temperance beers, wines and champagne were developed. Food was wide-ranging from full meals to snacks of plates of meat, cakes or bread and butter.

The Victorian temperance movement was well intentioned with many prominent members. Gladstone, Lord Shaftesbury and the Duke of Westminster all played a key role. Despite its good intentions, the coffee-house movement did not last. Poor management skills, with sponsors being unable to refrain from preaching to the clientele and the premises regularly being used for evangelical meetings, all proved unpopular. The most successful spin-off of the movement was the working-class cafés, with their straightforward, value for money approach.

The 1900s

The end of the 1800s saw a rapid expansion in the growth of pubs and breweries, which ended in a slump in the early 1900s as property values plummeted, leaving widespread bankruptcies and a lack of investment in redecorating and rebuilding. The major players, with an increasing monopoly of licensed premises lacked the capital for investment.

The reputation of the pub was changing as the emphasis on drinking socially changed. Beer gardens were increasing, women were encouraged to visit pubs with their husbands, the provision of meals increased and soft drinks became available. The gin palaces became more akin to pubs with gin consumption decreasing and customers demanding a larger choice of beverages. Museums, galleries, libraries, swimming pools and football matches were now alternative social centres. The new image gave respectability to the licensed trade.

The outbreak of the First World War led to the military authorities requesting restrictions on opening hours primarily to prevent servicemen being entertained by civilian friends. The first step was closing pubs at 11.00 p.m., one-and-a-half hours earlier than previously. This did not prevent customers from starting their drinking sessions at 5.00 a.m. in London and 6.00 a.m. elsewhere. The government set up a Liquor Control Board in May 1915 in response to criticism that war production was being affected as a result of excessive consumption of alcohol by many of the workers. Morning and afternoon closing periods were introduced. 'Convictions for drunkenness in England and Wales fell from 183,828 in 1914 to 29,075 in 1918' (Barr, 1995: 140).

The controls introduced in the First World War proved to have a beneficial effect, and therefore there was a reluctance to restore the restrictions to peacetime levels. The major defect with the principle of early closing, was pointed out to the Royal Commission by a Mr A. Reade who explained:

> that during the last few minutes before closing time customers may be seen clamouring at the bar to gulp down two or three drinks, where, in a free country across the channel, they would have been perfectly content to sit at their leisure over one. Early closing, in other words, was counter-productive. (Barr, 1995: 141)

The opening hours were not significantly changed from 1918 until the 1987 licensing bill.

Summary propositions

1 The history of drink and inns is synonymous with the development of most societies. As the society develops so do the complexities of the public house, inn and even non-alcoholic movement.

2 Many of the problems associated with alcohol in modern society are not new and since the fourteenth century in Islamic countries and the seventeenth century in Britain governments, religious movements and society as a whole have attempted to address these problems, with mixed success.

3 The British 'inn' is rich with history and worthy of detailed study in itself. At the beginning of the twenty-first century we find ourselves in a time when many of the decorative themes in houses and the range of food provided is returning to those of an earlier era.

Summary questions

1 Why has there always been resistance to the drinking of alcohol?

2 Why has ale or beer rather than wine been the drink of the British?

3 How have governments attempted to curb alcohol abuse?

4 Why were coffee houses sometimes seen as bad as alehouses for causing problems?

Case study

In your local area map the local hostelries. Define the buildings and names. Which are buildings of a bygone era, which are modern brick-built drinking houses, which have been converted from other uses? Examine the names and symbols used on the houses, their décor, and range of food and drink. Can you imagine any of them as the gin palaces, inns or hostelries of a previous era?

References and further reading

Barr, A. (1995). *Drink an Informal Social History.* Mackays of Chatham.

Girouard, M. (1990). *Victorian Pubs.* Yale University Press.

Hackwood, F. W. (1994). *Inns, Ales and Drinking Customs of Old England.* Guernsey Press.

Spiller, B. (1972). *Victorian Public Houses.* David & Charles.

CHAPTER 2

The modern industry

Section 1: The facts and figures

Turnover

> Our industry is set to become Britain's biggest industry – bigger than all UK manufacturing combined . . . we employ two-and-a-half million people, many in highly skilled and innovative jobs.
>
> Where else can people get their first step on the ladder to a career in retail management paying upwards of £40 000?
>
> Students value the importance of flexible and multi-skilled employment. This is something we most certainly provide – with the additional benefit that many of the skills acquired within our industry are directly transferable to other sectors. Increasingly people are turning to our industry for a career, not just a summer job. (Sir Ian Prosser, chairman of Bass plc, the UK's biggest pub operator; *Leisure Careers UK* [*LCUK*], October–November 1998: 5)

> Hospitality is one of the UK's largest industries, with over 260 000 hotels, restaurants and cafes, pubs and clubs, conference venues and other commercial establishments, and an estimated 100 000 catering outlets. (British Hospitality Association [BHA] web site)

> The Value of pub Catering grew by 24% between 1993 – 1997, from £3.35 billion to £4.14 billion making it the most popular eating out market in the UK. (*LCUK*, October–November 1998: 8)

	£bn	Index	£bn at 1993 prices	Index
1993	21.0	100	21.0	100
1994	21.6	103	21.1	101
1995	22.1	105	20.8	99
1996	22.5	107	20.7	99
1997	23.0	110	20.6	98
1998	23.2	111	20.1	96

Source: Mintel Pub Catering, October 1998. Mintel Marketing Intelligence Service. www.mintel.co.uk

Table 2.1
Trends in total UK pub market turnover, 1993–8

The UK pub market has increased sales by 11 per cent between 1993 and 1998, despite the pub outlets decreasing by 6 per cent. This highlights the increase in the average pub takings, which is now estimated at £5 700 weekly.

The number of pubs has declined, but the amount of investment in the development of new premises is high, with £800 million invested in restoration and renovation of premises in 1996 alone. The trend is to develop new premises towards the growth sectors, which are the young, the affluent and the family. Traditional male, blue-collar workers are declining in numbers, and pubs no longer want to be seen as purely drinking venues, with the turnover now less dependent on wet sales. Brewer landlords all report a better growth from their food sales.

Table 2.2 gives an indication of the growth areas in the pub market – alcoholic drink accounts for 59 per cent of turnover, value sales have increased by only 3 per cent between 1993 and 1997.

Catering sales have increased significantly by 23 per cent since 1993, with the majority of pubs offering competitively priced meals. 'Other' activities account for 15 per cent of total income, with the increasing revenue from accommodation, telephones, vending machines and gaming machines.

	1993 (£m)	%	1995 (£m)	%	1997 (£m)	%	% change 1993–7
Alcoholic drinks	13 224	63	13 685	62	13 580	59	+3
Catering	3 358	16	3 752	17	4 143	18	+23
Soft drinks	1 679	8	1 766	8	1 841	8	+10
Other*	2 729	13	2 869	13	3 452	15	+27
Total	20 990	100	22 072	100	23 017	100	+10

* E.g. gaming machines, accommodation, telephones, vending, etc.
Source: Mintel Pub Catering, October 1998. Mintel Marketing Intelligence Service. www.mintel.co.uk

Table 2.2
Breakdown of total pub turnover by major sector

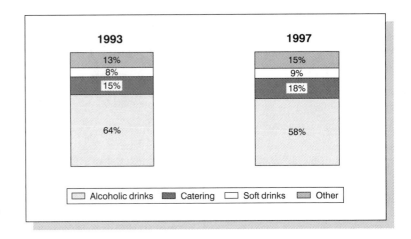

Figure 2.1
Pub turnover by sector, 1993 and 1997
Source: Mintel Marketing Intelligence.

The increase in food sales has increased the daytime turnover, as well as increasing weekend turnover, with the weekend meals turnover frequently subsidizing poor midweek sales. The value of pub catering has increased to 30 per cent between 1993 and 1998, with annual rates of growth currently in the region of 6–8 per cent. The eating-out market is estimated at £4.4 billion in 1998.

	£m	Index	£m at 1993 prices	Index
1993	3358	100	3358	100
1994	3568	106	3424	102
1995	3752	112	3452	103
1996	3934	117	3481	104
1997	4143	123	3541	105
1998	4414	131	3627	108

Table 2.3
The value of the eating-out market

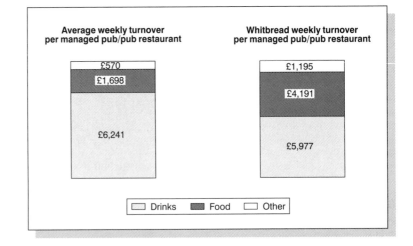

Figure 2.2
The industry and Whitbread approach to catering sales

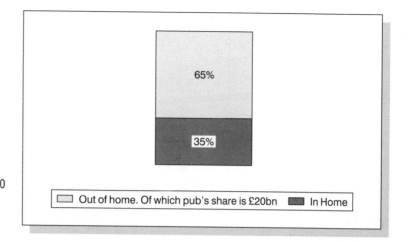

Figure 2.3
Public house share of the £130
billion UK leisure market
Source: Henley Centre and
industry estimates, June 1998.

'The fastest growing industry within the UK's biggest employer
and will provide one in five of all new job vacancies. Within the
fast-growing pub retailing sector alone, 230,000 vacancies will be
created by the year 2002' (*Whitbread PLC, Briefing Book*).

But not only is the overall volume changing but so is the way
in which we use our leisure time. The licensed house is one of the
major venues for leisure provision.

The markets that pubs traditionally cater for, those concerned
primarily with local usage are also changing. The three markets
of community (local usage), destination (those travelling to a
particular location for social purposes) and food (those using a
public house for eating out purposes) are still present but many
companies now aim for, and have achieved, a different balance
between these markets.

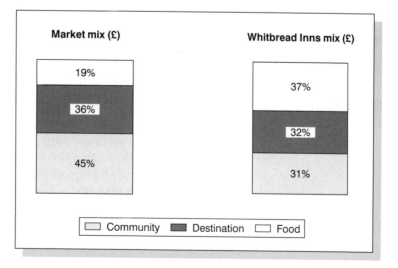

Figure 2.4
UK pub market dynamics:
Whitbread compared to overall
industry
Source: Henley Centre and
Whitbread, June 1998.

	%
All pubs	5
Community pubs	-3
– Family	15
Standard	-5
Destination pubs	4
Female friendly	15
Traditional	4
Young	-6
Food pubs	26
Adult	30
Family	17

Table 2.4
Pub market growth: the next five years

Profit sector	1981	Share %	1995	Share %	1996	Share %	1997	Share %	Growth %, 1996–7
Hotels	55 474	24.65	60 599	27.74	60 740	27.97	60 861	28.00	0.20
Restaurants	14 952	6.65	15 952	7.30	15 920	7.33	15 925	7.00	–
Fast food	539	0.24	1 613	0.74	1 770	0.82	1 913	10.00	8.10
Cafés and takeaways	34 204	15.20	31 518	14.43	30,990	14.27	30 369	14.00	(2.00)
Pubs	77 672	34.50	60 415	27.66	58 980	27.16	57 408	27.00	(2.70)
Travel	816	0.36	1 268	0.58	1 290	0.59	1 313	1.00	1.80
Leisure	41 414	18.40	47 083	21.55	47 475	21.86	47 912	22.00	0.90
Total	225 073	100.00	218 448	100.00	217 165	100.00	215 701	100.00	(0.70)

Source: Foodservice Intelligence.

Table 2.5 Number of outlets in profit sector, 1981–97

Contribution

In 1996, overseas visitors spent £13.6 billion in the UK excluding fares to UK carriers (a further £3 billion). This is set to grow to £20 billion by 2000. Hospitality accounts for 25% of our foreign invisible earnings. It earns more from exports than North Sea oil, financial services or civil aviation. (BHA Web site)

The country earns £26 for every £1 of government funding for the British Tourist Authority.

'Pubs serve
28 million meals
per week.'

Source: Barzone 1998

'Britain's pubs
sell over £10 billion
worth of beer
each year.'

Source: BLRA 1998

Pub Chain JD Weatherspoon
has won the NatWest Sunday
Times Business Enterprise
Award beating more than 400
companies across all industrial
sectors in the UK. The award is
given to the companies
showing significant
achievement in creating
employment, wealth and for the
enterprise shown in design,
manufacture and marketing of
products and services.

Source: LCUK 1998

Figure 2.5
Highlighting the importance of
the licensed trade industry to
the UK economy.

The licensed retail industry represents approximately 3%
of UK gross domestic product (GDP) and several
operators feature in the FTSE 100; these include Bass,
Scottish & Newcastle, and Whitbread, all capitalised at
several billions of pounds. (*LCUK*, October–November
1998)

Employment

Hospitality is employing 10 per cent of the total UK workforce,
approx. 2.5 million people. 'The industry is currently providing
one in five new jobs and the Henley Centre for Forecasting
estimates that the industry will generate an additional 400 000
new jobs by 2006' (BHA web site).

Employment in the UK hospitality industry can be divided
into two categories:

1 *Hospitality businesses* (hotels, restaurants, pubs, clubs and bars
and contract catering). Businesses account for two-thirds of all
the industry.

2 *Hospitality services* (hospitals, food outlets with a factory, etc.).
This remaining third of the industry are organizations whose
primary function is not in hospitality.

The total employment figure for Great Britain in 1998 was
1 880 000, with pubs, clubs and bars sector being the largest
employer with almost 400 000 employees, representing 35 per
cent of the overall workforce.

	1998
Hotels	259 000
Restaurants	332 000
Pubs, clubs and bars	399 000
Contract catering	150 000
Self-employed	123 000
Total hospitality businesses	1 263 000
Medical	231 000
Education	159 000
Industrial	95 000
Retail trade	65 000
Culture/sports	43 000
Public administration	15 000
Transport	9 000
Total hospitality services	617 000
Total overall	1 880 000

Source: Annual Employment Survey (1996)/Labour Force Survey.

Table 2.6
Total hospitality employees by sector, 1998

In the pubs, clubs and bars sector the ratio of employees to business declined from 5:1 to 4:1. The number of pubs, clubs and bars actually grew during this period, indicating that businesses are employing fewer people. Within the sector, the proportion of businesses employing between one and ten staff had increased from 83 per cent in 1991 to 85 per cent in 1998 (Hospitality Training Foundation, 1999).

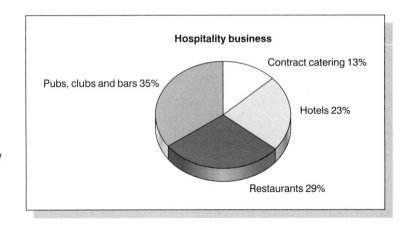

Figure 2.6
Percentage of employment by sector, 1998
Source: Annual Employment Survey, 1996, and Labour Force Survey, 1998.

Age ranges	16–19	20–24	25–29	30–39	40–49	50–59	60–64	65+
Sectors	%	%	%	%	%	%	%	%
Hotels	18	17	12	18	13	16	3	3
Restaurants	29	15	13	19	13	8	2	1
Bars, pubs and clubs	25	18	10	17	13	13	2	2
Catering	5	7	8	33	24	18	3	2
GB average	5	9	12	27	23	18	4	2

Source: Hospitality Training Foundation, 1999.

Table 2.7 Age analysis of employees per sector

Age

The licensed trade employs a significantly younger staff than the national average.

Bars, pubs and clubs have a very high percentage of young employees. Fifty per cent of the British workforce in 1998 was aged between thirty and fifty years compared to 30 per cent in bars, pubs and clubs. Given the skills shortages, the industry should be addressing the imbalance.

Full-time and part-time employment

Pubs, clubs and bars are dominated by part-time staff, with the highest ratio of part time to full time for any hospitality sector. This is due to both the type of working conditions found in the industry in terms of weekends and long hours and the need for flexibility (see Chapter 6).

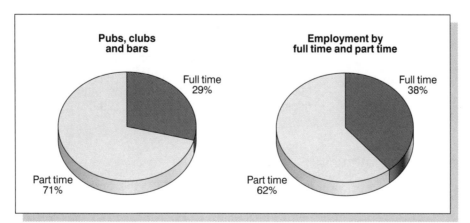

Figure 2.7 Employment for the UK hospitality industry
Source: Annual Employment Survey, 1996, and Labour Force Survey, 1998.

Gender

As shown in Table 2.8 female employees dominate the workforce in pubs, clubs and bars – 68 per cent, the average for the hospitality business sector being 66 per cent. The largest proportion of female employees is a staggering 93 per cent, within the education area of the hospitality services sector.

	Male	%	Female	%	Total
Hotels	102 000	39	157 000	61	259 000
Restaurants	111 000	33	221 000	67	332 000
Pubs, clubs and bars	129 000	32	270 000	68	399 000
Contract catering	37 000	29	90 000	71	127 000
Business sector total	379 000	34	739 800	66	1 117 000
Medical	31 000	14	200 000	86	231 000
Education	11 000	7	149 000	93	160 000
Industrial	39 000	41	56 000	59	95 000
Retail	11 000	17	54 000	83	65 000
Culture/sport	15 000	35	28 000	65	43 000
Public administration	7 000	49	8 000	51	15 000
Transport	5 000	51	4 000	49	9 000
Services sector total	119 000	19	498 000	81	618 000

Source: Annual Employment Survey, 1996, and Labour Force Survey, 1998.

Table 2.8 Gender variations in hospitality occupations

Within each hospitality occupation, there were wide variations in the percentage of male and female employees. At a managerial level, the industry saw a slightly higher percentage of males in employment than females [as shown in Table 2.8].

However, females stood a better chance of reaching management level jobs in hospitality than in other industries. With the exception of restaurant managers, publicans and hotel porters, female employees outnumbered male employees in all other occupations. (Hospitality Training Foundation, 1999)

Employment by ethnicity

As demonstrated in Table 2.10, the licensed trade is underrepresented with non-white employees at management level. Overall the hospitality workforce has twice the representation of non-white workers, which perhaps is not surprising given the large number of ethnic restaurants.

	Male %	Female %
Managers and administrators	67	33
General managers: government and large organizations	66	34
Production managers: manufacturing etc.	93	7
Financial and office managers etc	44	56
Managers in farming, horticulture etc.	85	15
Hotel and accommodation managers	47	53
Restaurants and catering managers	55	45
Publicans, club stewards etc.	59	41
Chefs/cooks	48	52
Waiters/waitresses	25	75
Bar staff	37	63
Housekeepers (non-domestic)	2	98
Hotel porters	96	4
Kitchen porters	34	66
Catering assistants	18	82
Cleaners, domestics	19	81

Source: Labour Force Survey, 1998.

Table 2.9 Percentage of employees by gender and occupation, 1998

	White (%)	Non-white (%)
Great Britain workforce	95.1	4.9
Hospitality workforce	89.2	10.8
Managers and proprietors in service industries	92.5	7.5
Hotel and accommodation managers	100.0	0
Restaurant and catering managers	84.2	15.9
Publicans, club stewards etc	97.7	2.3
Chefs/cooks	87.5	12.5
Waiters/waitresses	92.3	7.8
Bar staff	98.1	1.9
Housekeepers (non-domestic)	95.6	4.4
Hotel porters	92.3	7.7
Kitchen porters	91.2	8.8
Catering assistants	90.5	9.5

Source: Labour Force Survey, 1998.

Table 2.10 Percentage of employment by ethnicity, 1998

Employment by disability

Disability, as defined by the Labour Force Survey, covered the health problem that an individual suffered from – the health problems or disabilities connected with arms/hands, legs/feet, back/neck, seeing, hearing, speech impediment, skin/allergies,

Sector	% of workforce with a health problem that lasted over 12 months	% of workforce with a health problem that affects kind of work that they might do*	% of workforce with a health problem that affects amount of work that can be done*
All industries	15.9	6.7	4.6
Total hospitality	15.0	7.2	4.7
Hotels	15.7	7.9	5.0
Restaurants	18.4	7.8	5.0
Pubs, clubs and bars	13.5	6.4	4.2
Contract catering	16.4	6.7	4.6

Note: * Base: all those who had a health problem lasting more than twelve months.
Source: Labour Force Survey, 1998.

Table 2.11 Percentage of workforce affected by a health problem, 1998

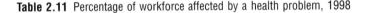

chest/breathing, heart/blood pressure, stomach/digestion, diabetes, depression/nerves, epilepsy, learning difficulties, mental illness, progressive illness or other problems. It should also be noted that the social environment and perceptions of disability are also important factors that can affect the kind or amount of work a disabled person can undertake.

Overall, pubs, clubs and bars have a lower percentage of health problems than the total hospitality industry, and are well below the national average for all industries.

The licensed trade is well represented on the Employers' Forum for Disability, which was set up to promote and share best practice on the recruitment and retention of disabled employees, and training:

- Allied Domecq Leisure and inns

- Bass Plc

- Whitbread PLC. (Employers Forum for Disability, 1998).

Pub managers' salaries

'A survey commissioned by Leisure Careers in the UK (LCUK), a joint industry/government-funded careers promotion initiative established in March 1998, shows that pay and rewards packages for licensee professional have significantly outstripped their public image' (*LCUK*, October–November 1998: 2). The aim of the research, which had the full backing of the pub retail industry, was to establish and communicate the career opportunities at all levels in the licensed leisure industry.

Research compared the gross rates of pay with a range of other occupations as shown in Table 2.12.

Compare these figures – all before income tax and living expenses are deducted – with the result from the institute survey: 'Pub manager £352 unweighted, £512 weighted' (LCUK Research, 1998).

Occupation	Weekly gross pay (£)
Travel agency managers	320.60
Managers and proprietors in service industries	353.70
Primary education teachers	427.40
Secondary education teachers	460.50
Civil service executive officer	338.70
Computer operators	288.30
Bricklayers/masons	302.90
Builders/building contractors	301.30
Quantity surveyors	437.60
Personnel officers	379.00
Nurses	360.20
Fire service officers	393.10
Environmental health officers	452.80
Civil service administrative officers	225.80
Local government clerical officers	258.60
Biological scientists and biochemists	499.50
Mechanical engineers	536.40
Design and development engineers	495.70

Source: New Earnings Survey from the office of National Statistics, 1997.

Table 2.12
Salary league

Average earnings	£18 312 (£352 per week) or £26 624 (£512 per week) when weighted
Maximum average earnings	£35 561 (unweighted)
Average years of experience	4–5 years
Companies recruit managers aged	19–24 years and upwards
Managers worked on average	44+ hours a week
Promotion from within the company	36%
Top five company benefits available to managers:	
Companies offering annual bonus	71%
Pensions	55%
Sales/turnover-related commission	52%
Private health insurance	48%
Share options	42%

Source: *LCUK*, October–November 1998: 2.

Table 2.13 Weighted earnings

What pub managers really earn

The New Earnings Survey was not weighted in terms of accommodation, food, benefits or bonus potential.

Major players

'A total of 319 pub estate operators (company or brewer that owns a large number of pubs) exist in the UK, controlling 40 916 pubs, with other pubs, clubs and bars being run by independents (free houses that are individually owned and operated). The ten largest operators controlled 25 849 pubs' (Hospitality Training Foundation, 1999: 13).

Rank	Estate operators	No. of pubs
1	Nomura Principal Finance Group	5540
2	Whitbread	3670
3	Allied Domecq Retailing	3500
4	Scottish and Newcastle	2790
5	Bass Leisure Retail	2530
6	Punch Taverns/Wellington Pub Co.	2303
7	Enterprise Inns Plc	1823
8	Pubmaster Ltd	1550
9	Greene King Plc	1136
10	Wolverhampton and Dudley Breweries Plc	1007

Source: *Pub Industry Handbook*, 1999.

Table 2.14
Top ten pub estate operators, 1999

Pub estate operators are divided into the following categories:

- national brewers
- regional brewer
- independent pub operator.

Sectors of the licensed trade industry

The sectors of the licensed trade industry range from the local pub or basic 'boozer' to the high-status destination venue. Within this range various types of establishment can be found such as bars, clubs, nightclubs, taverns, inns, etc. The distinction between these sectors can be blurred as one sector overlaps into another, as also happens between restaurants, bars and pubs. The model in Figure 2.8 helps to illustrate this range and the sliding scale of the organizations within it.

Definitions

1 *The pub.* A local hostelry, it may range from a basic 'spit and sawdust boozer', where the locals outstare any stranger venturing over the doorstep, to a comfortable 'home from home'. Either way its basic purpose is to provide alcoholic refreshment and like-minded company to the local community, so that instead of sitting at home and watching the television, customers/regulars can walk down the road and socialize with others doing the same thing in familiar relaxing surroundings. The place to go out to without actually going out, where locals may have a special stool reserved for them at the bar, have their own drinking vessels, and never have to specify their drink because the landlord already knows it. Food is generally irrelevant.

	Pub	Tavern	Destination venue	Specialist venue
Rationale for use	Local	Nearby	Occasional/ social group specific	Image centred
Usage	Alcohol	Alcohol and food	Food and alcohol	Entertainment and alcohol
Criteria for choice	Simple and good value			Highly sophisticated/ transitory

Figure 2.8 Overview of the range of the licensed trade industry

2 *The tavern.* A place to go out to, but which does not take too much effort to get there, mentally or physically, either on foot or by some other method of transport: a place to meet friends. The impetus for going may range from 'there's nothing on the television tonight shall we go to ... instead?' to 'the sun's shining, it's a lovely day shall we drive out somewhere for lunch?' A convivial, inexpensive pub-based establishment in which food plays a lesser or greater role depending upon the situation, although it would generally always do Sunday lunch.

3 *The destination venue.* A destination venue is one which the customer has made an effort to get to, where they make a conscious decision that this would be where they want to go because of some particular quality or service provided by the venue. The consumer can be sure that there will be other like-minded people there. A family with young children is likely to decide that if the parents want to be able to eat out and relax while the children are entertained then a Brewers Fayre (Bass) with a Charlie Chalk's Fun Factory may be the ideal place to go. 'Grey' consumers (see Chapter 5) may well choose to go to a Golden Oak Inn (Allied Domecq) as these establishments are aimed specifically at the older market, and aim to provide good value for money for those living on a fixed income, or pension, in clean quiet surroundings. The eighteen to twenty-four age group is likely to be drawn by those venues which play loud contemporary music, and provide fashionable drinks, such as the It's a Scream Chain owned by Bass. Marsden's Pitcher and Piano chain could be seen as an example of the more discerning twenty-four to thirty-five age group market venue, offering stylish surroundings, wine based rather than beer, quality led rather than budget led. In many of these venues food is as important as drink, and non-alcoholic beverages as significant as alcoholic ones.

4 *The specialist venue.* These establishments are often at the cutting edge of fashion; going there makes a statement about who you are and your lifestyle values. These establishments are also often transient, and so the operator would normally require a capital investment payback over one year rather than the normal five-year period. Nightclubs, style bars, café bars, cigar clubs, microbrewery bars are all examples of this type of venue. Most are aimed at the high disposable income groups, both pre- and post-nesters, whose boredom and loyalty thresholds are very low and who regularly move on as a new venue or fashion emerges. The entertainment factor may be the beverages; it may also be food, the celebrities who use (or are reputed to use) the establishment, the music, live acts or simply being seen in the right place. Image and reputation are extremely important.

A single venue can obviously fall into, or be used by, more than one sector. For instance, a pub with a great riverside location, views and good food can be both a destination venue to some of its customers and a local to others living nearby. A real ale pub, listed by the Campaign for Real Ale (CAMRA), is often both a local and a specialist venue, and many café bars such as Whitbread's Rosie chain can be a simple destination venue by day and, then, as its attached nightclub comes on stream at night it changes into a specialist venue. It is important that the potential customer base is fully analysed before the image and market positioning of any venue is established. (See Chapter 5 for more information.)

Type of licensed enterprise

The four types of venue mentioned above are normally operated by one of four systems, and each of the systems can operate for any of the types of venue, as shown below.

Managed premises

A managed premises is normally owned by a chain and run on a day-to-day basis by a manager. All income generated by the business goes to the parent company, and the manager receives a salary, plus, usually, an income-related bonus. Managers do not own any part of the business, but neither do they have any risk, rather they work within guidelines set down by head office. Some people prefer to manage rather than risk ownership, others see management as a transitory phase, during which they are gaining valuable experience which they can ultimately use in their own future premises.

Tenancy

A tenancy occurs when a prospective landlord wants more 'ownership' of the business. They buy the tenancy from the outgoing tenant and or owner. A tenancy usually covers three, five or seven years and incoming tenants buy the fixtures and fittings, stock in trade and glasses. They would also be expected to put up a bond or security deposit. The bond is usually based on a week to a week-and-a-half's turnover. Incoming tenants would also need to have a certain amount of working capital, to carry them through until they have started to generate a sufficient income. The owner remains responsible for the building and its maintenance. If the owner of the tenancy is a brewery company, such as Bass or Brains, then tenants will be 'tied' into buying all their beer from the owning company, except for one guest ale. The owners make their money from the tenant's rent and the beer that they purchase. The tenant's profit is derived from the income of the establishment, plus any discount they receive on the beer that they are tied to purchase. However, it should be borne in mind that where the owning brewery gives a discount it is likely to be significantly less that the discounts that a non-tied house can obtain. A non-brewery tenancy is where the owner is not a brewing concern, such as Nomura the Japanese finance house. In this instance, although the parent company may not own a brewery, they will normally contract with a national brewery for that brewery to supply their tenants at a special discounted rate. The parent company will then derive its income from the tenant's rent, and discount rates on beer.

Leasehold

As with the tenancy there are also tied and non-tied leases, and again a tied lease links lessees to a brewery, whilst non-tied or free lessees can buy their beer from any source they choose. In many ways the purchase of a lease, which usually runs for anything between ten and twenty years, is similar to the purchase of any other freehold business. Potential lessees need to have worked out their business plan accurately, know where their capital will be coming from, calculated a realistic payback period, and know who between the lessees and the lessors is responsible for what parts of the maintenance of the property, etc. The main difference between a tied lease and a non-tied lease is that because tied lessees have to buy the majority of their beer from a specific brewery their rent will be lower than that of the non-tied lessee. The lessor probably makes the same amount of income in both cases, either from low rent plus beer sales, or from high rent. It is up to an incoming lessee to decide what type of lease they prefer.

Freehold

In this case the property is owned outright by the licensee/landlord and, as with any other business, they have the right to make a profit from any source that they see fit or, in this case, to buy from whichever supplier they choose to use. In this case, and especially, where an establishment has a very high turnover, the freeholder can often negotiate very good discounts from their suppliers, which may also include the loan of the very expensive beer dispense and line-cleaning systems, if draught ale is appropriate to the establishment. A freeholder is also likely to be able to negotiate substantial discounts from wholesalers for non-draught beer products. A freehouse is obviously much more expensive to buy than a leasehold property, but the bottom line is that all the profits of the business are retained by the owners. (They also shoulder all of the risk!)

The rationale behind the sectors

For those wanting to enter the licensed trade industry, it is beneficial to consider why one outlet might be operated as a tenancy and another very similar style operation, perhaps owned by the same company, might be managed. The vast majority of licensed trade premises within the UK are owned by a small number of regional and national chains. Most of these companies float their shares on the stock exchange, are responsible to their shareholders for how their (the shareholders') money is invested and for the return on investment that the shareholders receive. Shareholders may be private individuals or, especially in the very large companies, another company seeking to invest money to make future profits for their shareholders or members, i.e. most pension funds are supported by institutional share-buying in quoted companies such as those companies in the FTSE 100. These institutions invest to make money. If shareholders do not believe that they are maximizing their investments they will simply sell their shares in one business and buy shares in another. In extreme cases, this can leave the first company without the necessary financial backing to carry on business – they go bankrupt or are taken over by another more financially sound company.

For shareholders to have confidence in a business it helps if they understand what it is about and the philosophy that motivates the way that they trade. Nomura is currently the largest owner of on-trade premises in the UK, but the company is primarily a finance house – so why buy UK pubs? In simple terms many UK pubs are in prime city-centre locations and, therefore, in property terms, appreciation of capital, etc., they are good financial investments. Property, especially in Southeast England, is appreciating at a much higher rate than many other business investments at the end of the 1990s. Nomura is not in the least bit interested in running pubs or bars, therefore it has set up an operating division within the company whose purpose is to ensure, as far as possible, that these properties are run by tenants. The tenants do the day-to-day running of the business, and pay rent to Nomura. Nomura receives the rent and is also the sole owner of these properties and derives all the additional benefits of the rise in property values, while still staying true to their core business, finance.

There are other companies, especially brewery-based companies such as Bass, Whitbread, Wolverhampton and Dudley or Greene King for whom their *raison d'être* is traditionally the production and sale of alcoholic beverages. These companies need to have outlets for their beer, and other beverages. Since a large managed house might take £7000 or more per week, and a similar tenanted property only realize £1500 per week in rent, plus the owning company will retain much more control of the product/brand which is being sold in the managed house, many of the big chains prefer to manage the majority of their properties. This is particularly true in establishments such as nightclubs where draught beer is a minor part of the product sold. The parent company still makes profit from any beer sold, plus everything else.

However, it may be that the parent company is unable to have solely managed or solely tenanted premises no matter what the publicly stated aim of the company is. This is because there are still marginal properties in existence, usually acquired many years ago by one of the brewing-based companies, which now find themselves operating in a geodemographic environment which is distinctly different to when the property was first acquired. For instance a pub may have operated very success-fully as a local for a busy shipbuilding docks area. When the shipbuilding ceased, much employment ceased and the same pub now operates at a more marginal level for a predominantly unemployed community. However, government plans for inner-city regeneration, upmarket housing on brownfield sites, etc. mean that the owning company may decide to keep the property because the location would indicate that when the regeneration begins the pub will have the potential to be a very successful operation once again. These properties may be kept on the company's books, because they cannot sell them, or as a service to the community which keeps the company's name in front of a section of the population, or while the company waits for something like the inner-city regeneration plan to come into effect. In these cases, where the pub is only likely to succeed at the present time if a lot of onsite effort is put in, the company may prefer to have a tenant run the establishment on a fairly low, short-term, rent. The brewery will make income from the tenancy agreement, and the tied beer sales, without having the effort of actually managing the establishment.

Choosing a business and sources of finance

How do prospective landlords decide what type of business they would like to run, and how much control of the business do they want? Statistics show that well over 60 per cent of food and beverage businesses set up independently fail within their first year. There are of course many reasons for this, but the most common are that the owners do not understand the product that they are selling, the property is not in the correct location, the ethnic mix of the target population has not been analysed sufficiently and not enough capital has been raised at the beginning.

Experience helps to overcome the first two problems, hence the industry emphasis (reinforced in this book) on hands-on experi-ence. Actual experience helps the prospective landlord make realistic calculations about the amount of finance needing to be raised to acquire or start up a business with a good profit potential. Understanding how the industry works also increases the prospective landlord's ability to write a realistic business plan, to forecast their finances accurately for the next 3 years or so. Understanding the industry would also mean being aware, for instance, that a licensed business is unlikely to be as successful in an area, for example, with a large Muslim population, as it could be where the ethnic mix is different. In addition to this, whilst the prospective landlord is employed within the trade they should be able to create some capital of their own, via their salary, and build up an invaluable network of contacts for use when they step out on their own. A good track record will also help when going to a bank or brewery for a start-up loan.

Whilst banks are the obvious source of finance, when seeking to buy into a non-tied property, the large breweries should also be considered as a potential source of money. The large breweries are often happy to lend money on a sound business proposition, because they will also be able to tie the new owner into their beer. All prospective landlords should look at this option because although they may be tied to the brewery for their beer, the breweries often charge much lower rates on their loans than conventional sources of finance. Each situation needs to be looked at carefully, and the benefits of low interest rates plus beer tie weighed up against higher interest rates and free trade beer discounts.

An application for a new business may be stalled or refused by the local planning authorities as easily as by the local licensing magistrates. The local planning authorities may create restrictions as to what type of business may operate within specific areas of their district, and the local licensing magistrates may have regulations about what type of experience and qualifications an applicant must have before they will be granted a liquor licence. An initial visit to the appropriate planning office, and the local licensing clerk, may well save a lot of wasted time and money.

At all times the prospective landlord must have a good solicitor who understands the nuances of the licensed trade to ensure that the contract which is finally signed is the one that they intended to sign, whether taking over a new business or starting from scratch.

Summary propositions

1 The industry is a major one with a turnover in excess of £21 billion per annum.

2 The sector employs nearly 400 000 people directly; these are predominately part time and female.

3 Ownership of pubs and bars is split between individuals and groups. The groups are further split into breweries, pub companies and financial institutions.

4 There are four main sections, each containing different types of venue, and there are four main ways of administering these venues. Prospective landlords must be clear about what type of venue, and situated in which sector they want to run, and how they want to run it.

Summary questions

1 How has the source of revenue in licensed houses changed in the last ten years?

2 Why is the employment pattern the way it is in the sector, with particular emphasis on part-time workers and female employees?

3 How do the aims of the brewery-owned houses differ from those run by specialist pub companies?

4 Why is it advisable to gain hands-on experience before starting the process to run your own establishment?

5 What type of business do you want to run? Why?

6 How will you finance this business?

Case study

The J. D. Weatherspoon chain of themed venues has decided to open more outlets during the year 2000 and will create approximately 3000 new jobs in these units. This follows a number of years of extensive growth for the company, which provides an extensive range of drink and food without the distraction of television, pool tables or video games.

1 Why has the company decided to expand now and on such a grand scale?

2 What is it about the industry, its market and its profit potential that has led to such an expansion programme?

3 What is going to be the effect of these new units on the local business environment?

References and further reading

British Hospitality Association (BHA) (1999). *Trends and Statistics.* BHA.

British Institute of Innkeeping *Leisure Careers UK.* Bi-monthly newsletter.

Caterer and Hotelkeeper (journal).

Employers Forum for Disability (1998) in *Labour Market Intelligence.* Hospitality Training Foundation.

Hospitality Training Foundation (1999). *Key Facts and Figures for the Hospitality Industry.* Hospitality Training Foundation.

Management of Licensed Houses. Croner Publications.

Mintel Marketing Intelligence (1998, 1999). www.mintel.co.uk

Pub Industry Handbook (1999). Quantum Publishing Ltd.

The Publican (journal).

Sargent, M. and Lyle, T. (1998). *Successful Pubs and Inns.* 2nd edn. Butterworth-Heinemann.

Whitbread PLC Briefing Book. Issue 13, (1999).

Williams, S. (1999). *Lloyds Bank Small Business Guide.* Penguin Books.

CHAPTER 3

The licensed enterprise and the law

Introduction

Most people, when they decide to make the licensed trade their career, do not have enough capital, experience or surety to buy their own business even though some types of enterprise do not require a large capital outlay, perhaps only £10 000 for a small tenancy. Many of them will work for a number of years for one of the chains of houses and then move on to some form of ownership which gives them more control of the business. Other, mature, people may have some form of capital, and have worked for some years in a managerial capacity within another industry, and would want to start at the ownership level.

No matter which route is used to enter the industry the impact of various types of legislation over recent years means that licensing magistrates and other official bodies such as the local planning authorities do not look kindly upon people with little or no licensed trade experience and may refuse to issue the all-important justices' licence if they consider an applicant has no understanding of the licensed trade. It is therefore recommended that the reader should have a good understanding of all the various types of licensed enterprise, and have a goal in mind with regard to the type of operation in which they are interested. However they should also gain some practical experience behind the bar. The prospective landlord should probably aim to start as a hands-on trainee manager for a major company, particularly one with a reputation for good management training schemes, such as Whitbread or Bass. The prospective landlord will then have a better understanding of which sector of the industry they feel comfortable working in, and what type of enterprise they want to operate, manage or own.

Liquor licences

Anyone intending to work in any supervisory, managerial or ownership capacity in any establishment where alcohol is sold must have a full working knowledge of the relevant aspect of current liquor licensing law. Justices licences are not granted to those without this knowledge and without the relevant licence alcohol cannot be sold. This section, which should only be considered to be an introduction to the most important aspects of liquor licensing, covers the main relevant Acts and extrapolates those aspects which affect the daily working life of a licensee. Most working licensees will also have access to Croner's *Management of Public Houses* or some similar publication which keeps them updated on relevant law, liquor licensing being just a part of this area. See the 'References and further reading' section at the end of the chapter for more information.

Licensing Act 1964 (England and Wales), Licensing (Scotland) Act 1976 and liquor licence applications

The Licensing Act of 1964 consolidated and rationalized all the licensing law that had predated it, and forms the basis for all current liquor licensing law. It also set up the current system for the issue, control and transfer of liquor licences. A licensing committee is set up, by the local magistrates' court (England and Wales) or licensing board (Scotland) on which between five and 15 Justices of the Peace sit. This committee must meet in the first fortnight in February and between four and eight times during the year. These are the sessions at which liquor licences are issued, revoked or transferred. At least eight weeks' notice must be given of each session, so that applicants have enough time to put in their applications and for any objections to new licences to be lodged. An applicant for a new licence must put a notice of their application in a local newspaper, notify the clerk to the licensing justices, the police and relevant local authorities in writing at least 21 days before the session. Applicants to transfer a licence need to inform the same bodies, in writing, as well as the existing licence holder. Groups who are likely to object to licences being issued or transferred are the police, on legal grounds; fire authorities, on safety grounds; local residents on nuisance grounds and local businesses for unfair competition. If anyone decides to object they will attend the court at the appropriate session and the magistrates will consider all the details before deciding whether or not to issue a liquor licence.

Refusal and restriction of licence

It should be noted that the licensing magistrates can refuse a licence application or impose restrictions on any type of licence which they decide to issue. The most likely circumstances for refusal are if:

- the licensee or the applicant is not considered to be a fit and proper person. Many magistrates make it a condition of issuing the licence that the applicant has the relevant British Institute of Innkeeping (BII) certificate to prove that they have a good understanding of current licensing law, and this applies both to new applicants and those applying to renew their licenses

- the magistrates feel that the premises are not used or intended to be used for the purpose stipulated in the licence

- the premises are unsuitable due to the risk of fire

- the premises have been altered since the last application, or differ from the plans of the premises submitted to the court and the court has not been notified of these changes *before* they were made

- the premises are being mainly used by unaccompanied persons who are under eighteen years of age

- the premises are being used for the sale of drugs

- the customary main meals are not being served (part IV licences)

- non-alcoholic drinks, including water, are not available.

Renewal

All licences have to be renewed at every third (triennial) General Annual Licensing Meeting in February as calculated from 1995, hence the February meetings have become known colloquially as the 'Brewster Session'. To reduce pressure on the system, all renewal applications can be made in writing, unless the licensee has received notification of an objection. In this case they must appear in person. The main licensing session is in February, all new or renewed licences starting from 5 April. If the licence is not renewed it automatically expires on 4 April.

Transfer

Many businesses open up at times of the year other than February, and licences are continually being transferred because of sales, death, etc. This is why there are other sessions throughout the year, known as Transfer Sessions. These other sessions allow the applicant to gain a licence to run their premises until the next Brewster Session, when they can apply for the usual triennial licence.

A liquor licence is granted to the licensee at a particular address. If the licensee moves on for any reason whatsoever, a new licence must be sought by the new person who is running the original establishment, and by the original licensee at their new place of work. This obviously has implications for the date on which a new owner/licensee takes over new premises, as the establishment can only operate legally if the correct licence and licensee is in place. An Interim Authority or Protection Order is generally sought to cover unplanned changes of licensee, and in most establishments two people are named as licensees, in case one leaves or dies, so that the business can carry on as usual until the next Transfer Session.

Licensing (Restaurant) Act 1987, Licensing Act 1988, Licensing (Sunday Hours) Act 1995

This series of amendments to the 1964 Act enabled alcohol to be served throughout the day in the UK (England and Wales following Scotland), and thus bought pubs and restaurants more in line with current consumer behaviour and the demands of the tourism industry. This extension to the permitted hours did not, as opponents had stated, cause alcohol consumption to rise within the UK. In fact per capita consumption of alcohol per annum has fallen slightly from 9.75 litres of pure alcohol (LPA) in 1988 to 9.64 (LPA) in 1998 (*The Drink Forecast*, vol. 19, no. 2) despite the longer permitted hours. Instead it has enabled industry and government to look at the whole liquor licensing system, as discussed towards the end of this chapter.

Permitted hours for on-licences (bars) and part IV licences (restaurants):

- Weekdays: 11 a.m. to 11 p.m.

- Sundays and bank holidays: 12 noon to 10.30 p.m.

- Christmas day (on-licences only): 12 noon to 3.00 p.m. and 7.00 p.m. to 10.30 p.m.

Drinking-up time:

- Pubs etc.: twenty minutes, the drinks having been bought within the permitted hours

- Restaurants etc.: thirty minutes the drinks having been ordered within the permitted hours.

The licensing magistrates have the right to alter these times if they feel that there is a need to do so. For instance, they may allow the establishment to open one hour earlier, at 10 a.m. or make them close for part or all of an afternoon. These variations, in opening/closing times, can be made for different days of the week, but the need for the variation must last for at least 8 weeks. The variation will be set at the licensing session and will apply throughout the duration of the licence. An alteration like this often applies in tourist areas, where publicans want to open longer during the season, or in towns that have a set market day when there are more potential customers around, or in a residential area, near a school perhaps. The need must exist before the application is made.

Children's Certificate 1996

This is the most recent amendment to be brought in, and allows parents and children to socialize publicly together more easily that in the past. The Children's Certificate applies mainly to public houses, because children have always been allowed into premises whose main purpose was the sale of main meals, however, it can also be applicable to some wine bars or café bars if there are no table meals or area set aside specifically for eating. It allows children under the age of fourteen and accompanied by an adult to enter licensed premises if the premises are suitable, and it brings the UK in line with most of the rest of Europe. However the premises have to be 'suitable', i.e. a pub with only one room where heavy drinking was encouraged, and/or had gambling machines, and/or no food was served would not be permitted a Children's Certificate. A pub which offered food and had more than one room, and therefore a room which could be set aside, with no gambling or smoking could apply. Where a Children's Certificate is in place the children must leave the premises by 9 p.m. although there is a thirty-minute 'eating up' time allowed.

Types of licences

Part IV licences

Briefly, restaurant and residential licences are known as 'part IV licences'. They can either be combined in one licence, for example, in a hotel with a restaurant open to the general public, or be applied for singly as for a stand-alone restaurant or a guesthouse with no externally accessible restaurant for instance. In some establishments, with several food and beverage outlets, restaurants, bars and nightclub, the management may need to apply for both part IV licences and on-licences.

The restaurant licence applies to establishments whose primary purpose is to provide main meals. This means that the meal must be a table meal, where a customer sits down at a table, or counter to eat their food. Therefore if there is a takeaway service people may not be served alcohol whilst they wait for their meals.

The residential licence is granted to those places whose main purpose is to provide accommodation and some food, i.e. breakfast, and at least one other main meal. It means that alcohol can be served to residents at any time of the day or night, because there are no permitted hours.

On-licences

This is the type of licence that a pub or wine bar might have, where the sole purpose of the business is to sell beverages, mainly alcoholic. A hotel may also apply for this type of licence if it has a bar that is open to, and used by, the general public.

The local magistrates can restrict an on-licence, or the applicant can apply for a restricted licence. The restrictions, which can also be applied to part IV licences, are as follows:

- Cider only – used mainly by cider producers themselves to encourage gate sales.

- Beer and cider only – rarely applied for.

- Beer, cider and wine – mainly applied for as a restriction to a restaurant licence in areas such as fast food where the profit comes from a quick turnover of customers.

- Wine only – used mainly by wine bars.

If there are no restrictions, and any type of alcohol can be sold then the licence is called a full on-licence. Pubs, café bars, cocktails bars, clubs will apply for this licence.

Off-licences

This is where alcohol is sold for consumption off the premises, i.e. in a supermarket, or 'off-licence'. Again there may be restrictions placed on the licence as described previously. The licensee may be entitled to sell all kinds of intoxicating liquor or restrict themselves to just beer, cider and wine. Some bars have a 'carry out' trade. They will then hold both on- and off-licences

Club licences

The clubs referred to here are not nightclubs (see the Special Hours Certificate), but member's clubs, usually with a social or sporting *raison d'être*. There are two main types of club which sell alcohol:

1 A licensed club is one which is operated by individuals or a limited company as a commercial enterprise where alcoholic drink is sold only to members, e.g., a 'gentleman's club'. This may take place at any time during their opening hours. Many clubs offer accommodation to their members, and so they may be residents and have residential rights.

2 A registered club is run by its own members, and the members own the stock of liquor. It must be a non-profit-making organization, and is often a sports club, the local football, or cricket club. Again the members set the times for the sale of liquor, which should reflect the purpose of the organization.

Extension licences

These may only be sought by someone with a part IV licence or an on-licence. The types of drinks that can be sold are the same as those of the main licence, therefore, if the licence has any restrictions these will also apply to the extension. Not all extensions are applicable to all establishments.

Occasional licence (on-licensed premises only) • • •

This is granted to licensees to enable them to sell liquor at a place other than the one they are licensed at normally. This is often for a social function, a twenty-first birthday party in a church hall, the beer tent at a fund-raising event, etc. It is usually granted for a one-off occasion, but may be issued for a maximum of 3 weeks in special circumstances, i.e. if a local club is putting on a Christmas show for several performances, and wants a refreshment bar during each. Twenty-four hours' notice of intention to apply must be given to the police, but the licensee will not have to appear in person to apply for the licence if 1 month's notice is given in a written application (two copies) to the clerk to the justices.

General Order of Exemption • • •

This would enable a licensee to open and close at different times from the normal permitted hours. It is only granted where there is an actual need already existing, i.e. in the immediate neighbourhood of a market or place where people follow another lawful calling. If the order is granted it will specify the permitted hours.

An example of this would be in London, at Smithfield Market, or Billingsgate. Here most business takes place between 2 a.m. when the market traders arrive and 10 a.m. when everybody is going home. If pubs, etc. could not open during these hours then they would go out of business. Also 9 a.m. to

10 a.m. is the end of the working day for the traders and they are as entitled to have a drink and meal at the end of their working day as anyone else.

Special Order of Exemption

This is an order which allows the licensee to extend their permitted hours to cater for a special external event. An example of this would be where an establishment was given permission to stay open all day and into the early hours of the following morning if there was a carnival being held locally on that day. Again the licensee cannot create the event, but can take advantage of it. Applications are made to the local magistrates' court, or the police in London, and sufficient notice of the application must be given.

Supper Hour Certificate

Where a licensed premises can prove that its main purpose it to provide 'substantial refreshments', that is to say, a proper meal which is eaten at a table with a knife and fork, it can apply for a Supper Hour Certificate. This applies to all restaurants, but it also applies to those pubs, bars and café bars with actual restaurants. The certificate has the effect of extending the opening hours by one hour, so that alcohol can be sold until 12 midnight (or 11.30 p.m. on Sundays, bank holidays, etc.). Places that take advantage of this type of licence are generally in urban areas with a large number of people around, for instance, those near cinemas, leisure complexes or nightclubs.

Extended Hours Certificate

Premises which have a Supper Hour Certificate can apply for an Extended Hours Certificate. This enables them to stay open for an extra hour, until 1 a.m. (excluding Sundays). However, in order to be able to apply, live musical entertainment must also be supplied and the liquor must be ancillary to both the food and entertainment provided. Justices can restrict this licence to certain days of the week if they feel that a nuisance might be caused to local residents. The most common restriction here is to allow the licence to operate only on Thursdays, Fridays and Saturdays. The establishment will also need a public entertainment licence, to enable live music to be played (see section on 'Entertainment licences' in this chapter).

Special Hours Certificate

Any premises which has a licence for music and dancing may apply for a Special Hours Certificate. They must also provide substantial refreshments. The permitted hours are then extended to 2 a.m. outside Central London and 3 a.m. within it. Permitted hours start at 6 p.m. and so this type of licence is typical of a commercial disco. During British Summer Time these hours are extended to 3 a.m. outside Central London and 4 a.m. inside. The licence may have restrictions placed on it; for example, it may only be valid for certain days of the week, again perhaps Thursday, Friday and Saturday. The closing hours may also be reduced to somewhere between midnight and 2 a.m., except in Central London where it can only be restricted to 2 a.m. Conversely the local magistrates can also extend them if a need is proven. Currently the government is considering a proposal to allow Special Hours Certificates to be issued on Sundays.

Entertainment licences

These are not liquor licences, but will be required if there is a Special Hours Certificate in force, and upon other occasions.

A public entertainment licence is required if:

- the general public, i.e. customers, can attend

- live music is provided by more than two performers

- dancing takes place

- karaoke is in place (a cinema licence may also be needed depending upon the type and output of the karaoke equipment).

Public entertainment licences are granted by the appropriate local council in London, and by the appropriate district council elsewhere. No public entertainment licences are issued for Sundays, although this, like so much licensing law, is currently under discussion.

If a licensee just provides background music in the form of radio, television, recorded sound, video and audio jukeboxes they will not need a public entertainment licence, but probably will need a Performing Right Society (PRS) licence for any live performance or public playing of copyright music and/or a Phonographic Performance Limited (PPL) licence for the public playing of recorded copyright music by record player, jukebox, compact disc (CD), tape recorder, etc.

A Video Performance Limited (VPL) licence is needed for the copyright content of videotapes, i.e. if they are used in video jukeboxes or with karaoke equipment, and under certain circumstances a cinema licence made be needed if the video is considered to be a film show. Licensees should always check with their local authorities exactly what licence is needed before going ahead with any entertainment, as fines for infringements of licences are currently up to £20000.

The whole system

Having begun to grasp the principles of current licensing legislation the reader may be pleased to know (and will undoubtedly concur) that the present industry and government view is that the whole system is too complex, and places unnecessary burdens on the licensee. Therefore, fundamental changes are being actively reviewed by the government. The main points currently being considered are that there would be two licences, a personal licence proving that the individual is suitable to work with alcoholic beverages, and the second a premises licence, proving that the premises are suitable for the sale of alcohol. The intention of the premises licence is that the premises would have whatever kind of licence is suitable for that establishment, be it late opening, children on site, types of alcohol sold, and so on. The personal licence would enable staff within the trade to move around without the enormous problems that are often currently caused when a licensee changes premises. It would also remove the need for public entertainment licenses, since the on-site activity would be incorporated in the premises licence.

A government White Paper on these issues is due to be published in 2000, and if passed the implications for the industry will be profound. Therefore, the author advises the reader to check with a solicitor knowledgeable about current licensing law, or one of the professional associations, as an important part of their business planning well before any contract is signed.

Weights and Measures (Various Foods) (Amendment) Order 1990

From 31 December 1994 imperial measures were no longer permitted within the UK, except for the sale of draught beer. All other alcoholic beverages had to be sold in measures which were standardized throughout the European Union (EU). These measures are as follows:

1 *Draught beer and cider* must be sold in multiples of a third or a half of a pint or multiples of half a pint. All glasses must either have a line indicating the level of a pint or half a pint, be an exact pint or half a pint, or the pumps must be metered. Current good practice recommends that in brim measure glasses when the head has collapsed the glass should be at least 95 per cent full.

2 *Bottled or canned beer and cider* are sold in various amounts, and these amounts must be clearly visible on the container. The customer must be served with a can or bottle specifically opened for that sale.

3 *Spirits* must either be sold in a sealed bottle or in multiples of 25 or 35 millilitres. (This last measure is uncommon in England and Wales but is the standard in much of the rest of the EU.) Only one of these measures may be used in any establishment.

These measures apply to gin, whisky, rum and vodka, but not if there are more than three different drinks in the glass. The drink is then classed as a cocktail and can be free poured. These measures also do not apply if the customer specifies another proportion in a mixed drink, but in reality most establishments vary the mixer measure rather than the spirit measure for costing purposes if they receive this type of request.

4 *Wine*:
(a) Bottled wine must be sold in bottles of 75 cl, or multiples of 25 cl, i.e. one-and-a-half litres.
(b) Carafes of wine must be sold in multiples of 25 cl, and the carafe size must be clearly stated for the customer to read before purchasing.
(c) Glasses of wine must be sold in quantities of 125 ml or 175 ml or multiples thereof, and all free pour glasses must have measure lines marked on them. The establishment must state which size glass it is using, usually on the price list.

There are no prescribed measures for other spirits, aromatized wines, liqueur wines or liqueurs. However, for cost and control purposes most establishments use a 50 ml measure for their aromatized and liqueur wines, martinis, sherries, ports, etc., and a 25 ml measure for all other spirits and liqueurs, i.e. brandy, Bailey's and Archers.

Notices that must be displayed

To enable the customer to make decisions about the type of establishment they are going into, what types of drink are being sold, the opening hours, the size and cost and therefore the value for money of the beverages, all establishments must display various notices. The notices should be prominently displayed and easy for the customer to read. If these notices are not displayed the establishment is in contravention of its licence, whatever kind it holds. The notices are as follows:

- the name of the licensee

- the type of licence and any extensions or restrictions

- any entertainment licence which is in force

- the under eighteen drinking law

- the Weights and Measures (Various Foods) (Amendment) Order 1990

- the sizes of the basic measures used in the establishment

- bar prices, or a representative sample of them if more than thirty different drinks are sold, inclusive of value added tax (VAT)

- the alcohol volume of the drinks, or a representative selection of them if more than thirty different drinks are sold

- a notice prohibiting the sale of tobacco to young persons (if tobacco is sold on the premises).

It is illegal to sell alcohol beverages to young persons under the age of 18.

Figure 3.1
Example of one of the notices that must be displayed on licensed premises

Young persons (assuming that there is no Children's Certificate in place), general points

Under five

It is an offence to give alcohol of any sort to a child under five except on doctor's orders, or in a medical emergency.

Five to fifteen

Children between these ages may drink alcoholic drinks at home or in a restaurant with a meal, but cannot buy it or be served by employees of the establishment. This means that a parent or guardian can give a child some of their drink if they choose to do so, but anyone not acting *in loco parentis* would be acting illegally.

Specific points related to liquor licences

Under fourteen

It is an offence to allow children under the age of fourteen into licensed premises during permitted hours, unless a Children's

Certificate has been obtained. There are some exceptions to this rule:

- the child is the child of the licensee
- the child is resident on the premises, i.e. in a hotel
- the child is only in the bar to pass from one place to another and there is no other route, i.e. the child is going from the garden to the toilet
- if the sale of liquor is ancillary to the purpose of the establishment, i.e. the bar on a railway station platform.

Fourteen to seventeen

Young people may be allowed on to licensed premises, at the licensee's discretion, but may not purchase or consume alcohol, except in the following circumstance:

1 People aged sixteen or seventeen may purchase beer, cider or perry if it is to be consumed ancillary to a main meal, and if they are eating in a part of the establishment exclusively set aside for the purpose of service of meals.

2 With the exception of the above, it is illegal to allow a person who is under the age of eighteen to buy and consume alcohol on a licensed premises.

It is also illegal to employ anyone under the age of eighteen to work in on-licensed premises in any capacity connected with the service of alcoholic drinks, unless they are on a bona fide training scheme. Between the ages of sixteen and eighteen if a young person is on an approved training scheme, such as a modern apprenticeship, then they may work behind a bar as long as they are supervised by the licensee or an appropriate person. The licensee must tell the police that they will be taking part in the scheme, and the young person may not work outside general licensing laws. In general, though, the bureaucracy caused by having an under-eighteen modern apprentice often means that most busy landlords are not interested in employing those under eighteen years of age behind the bar.

In a restaurant, or where there is a part IV licence in place, a person between the ages of sixteen and seventeen may take orders, serve and take payment for alcoholic beverages as long as this is just as a part of their main function, which is to serve meals at the table.

If liquor is sold to persons under the age of eighteen (except for the one exception given above), unless the licensee can prove that neither they nor their staff had any means of knowing that the person was under eighteen they will be fined, and if it happens again may lose their licence permanently. The under-age drinker is also liable to prosecution. Work is currently being undertaken by the government as well as associations such as the Portman Group to introduce identity cards that help to reduce this problem.

Gaming, betting and lotteries

1 Only games of skill are allowed, i.e. darts and snooker, without a specialist licence.

2 If gaming machines are installed there are three permitted types: amusement machines, quiz machines and amusement with prize (AWP) machines. However, certain types of establishment can make a significant part of their income from gaming machines.

3 Gaming must not be used to attract customers.

4 Betting is not permitted.

5 Lotteries can be held, but the law on lotteries is quite complex, and licensees should check exactly what the local regulations are before allowing any lotteries to take place on their premises.

6 Where betting and gaming are the main purpose of the establishment, i.e., it is a casino, a gaming licence is needed before a liquor licence can be obtained. This is a very specialist area and a potential operator in this area should take detailed, specialist advice before going any further.

Licensee rights and duties

A licensee has the right to refuse to sell alcohol to anyone. They do not have to give a reason, as it is often impossible to reason with a drunk. If the person refuses to accept the situation they are technically trespassing. If they become violent or disorderly the police can be called to remove them by force. Care must be taken, however, when refusing to serve people, to ensure that other laws, e.g., Race Relations and Sex Discrimination Acts, have not been broken by doing so. For further discussion in this area, see Chapter 8.

The licensee has a duty to maintain an orderly house especially in regard to the following:

1 It is an offence to sell alcohol to a drunken person.

2 It is an offence to allow drunken or violent behaviour.

3 It is an offence to allow your staff to do either of the above.

Prostitutes

Prostitutes may not work on or from licensed premises. Having said that, this is not generally a problem in the on-trade, although it can be in some hotels. If prosecuted, especially for a second offence, the licensee is likely to be charged with keeping a brothel. This is likely to cause a licensee to lose his or her licence permanently.

Exclusion Order

If someone persistently causes a licensee problems in their establishment they may apply to the magistrates' court for an Exclusion Order. This is an order which can be used against anyone who commits a violent act, or who threatens to do, or is likely to cause someone else to be violent. It excludes them from the named premises for anything from 3 months to 2 years depending upon the problem. People who break the order are liable to be fined or to be sent to prison. If a licensee has an Exclusion Order confirmed against someone, they will often warn other local licensees so that they can take steps to ensure that the problem customer does not decide to cause trouble in another establishment in the vicinity.

Vicarious liability

This means that the licensee is responsible for any offences committed by their employees, e.g., watering down the drinks, knowingly selling to under-age drinkers. The licensee would have to prove that they had exercised 'due diligence' to make sure that the premises were run properly. If an employee is found guilty of an offence and the licensee is held not to have exercised due diligence then the licensee may be disqualified from holding a licence for up to 5 years.

Rights of entry

Police officers have the right of entry at any time during permitted hours, and up to half an hour afterwards. However:

1 It is an offence to allow a constable in except as part of their duty, i.e., they could not take shelter in the event of a sudden cloud burst.

2 It is an offence to supply alcohol to a constable on duty, unless a senior officer permits it.

Customs and excise officers have the right to enter licensed premises and remove goods that are liable for forfeiture, i.e., fraudulent goods, if the drink is watered down or if the correct duty has not been paid on some of the alcoholic beverages, tobacco items, etc., for sale in the bar. If they enter the premises at night they must be accompanied by police officers.

Environmental health officers have the right to enter premises under various food safety acts. If they are dissatisfied with the safe and hygienic provision of food, or any other consumable, e.g., ice, they can either close the premises immediately or issue an improvement notice. For further details see Chapter 5.

Credit sales

It is an offence to give credit for liquor consumption on the premises, although not for off-sales. You must pay as you order and a till receipt should be given to confirm prices charged and payment given. This is to protect customers, especially drunken ones, from spending more than they have on them or from being overcharged. The two exceptions are:

- liquor which is to be consumed with a meal, and will be paid for at the end of the meal

- if the liquor is sold to a resident, they may sign for it and put the charge on their main bill.

It is now generally accepted, in principle, that credit and debit cards can be used as payment for alcoholic drinks – not to run up a tab, but round by round. Not all pubs and bars have credit card facilities because credit card companies charge commission on each transaction (see Chapter 7) and there has been little history/ demand for payment by this method. However, where food is a significant part of the licensee's income or where smart cards can be purchased which allow children and others to take advantage of various amusements provided on site to the limits of that card, etc., licensees are increasingly seeing the need to make credit or debit facilities available.

Summary propositions

1 This chapter contains a summary of current licensing law and not the fine detail. These regulations are constantly being monitored and updated. There can also be variations on the basic legislation given above which have been agreed by the local magistrates' court that in some way enhance or 'fit' local requirements following custom and practice. Potential licensees need to constantly update their knowledge and take advice from their solicitor before applying for the appropriate liquor licence/s.

2 Most licensing committees now require potential licensees to provide proof of their knowledge and application of current, relevant licensing law before they will issue a liquor licence. There are various qualifications that can be taken to provide this proof see (Chapter 9).

Summary questions

1 Why is it advisable to gain hands-on experience before starting the process to run your own establishment?

2 Are you eligible to be given a justices licence?
   (a) Have you got the correct qualifications to be awarded a liquor licence?
   (b) Are the premises suitable to be used for the sale of alcohol?

3 Have you checked with your solicitor about any recent changes with regard to liquor licensing law that may affect your application?

4 Do you know what type of licence you want to apply for?

5 Will the licence be suitable if your business expands in the way that you would like it to?

Case study

Certain areas of Liverpool have, along with several other traditional mercantile ports, been designated as areas in need of urban regeneration schemes. The traditional heavy industry of the city no longer exists, and other sources of employment must be found to regenerate the area. One such area within Liverpool is the area surrounding the old docks. Most of the original structures were destroyed by bomb damage during the Second World War, and the subsequent collapse of the local industry ensured that very little rebuilding took place. There is now just one traditional pub in existence within the docks area. However, under the regeneration scheme many new restaurants and café bars along with high tech/service industry businesses are due to open along the old

quays. This should create a dynamic alternate business, shopping and leisure area complementing the very crowded city centre.

1 What actions, particularly with regard to liquor licensing, is the current landlord/ owner of the one traditional pub left in the area likely to have to take into account to ensure that the establishment will be successful in its new environment and retain a unique selling point?

2 When the licensee is considering the new entertainment, new products, new drinking and eating styles in the area and potentially increased hours, which aspects of the licensing laws will need to be looked at in great detail?

References and further reading

Green, L., Mehigan, S., Phillips, J. and Stevens, L. (eds) (1998). *Patersons Licensing Acts*. 106th edn. Butterworth Shaw.

Management of Public Houses, Croner Publications.

National Licensee's Certificate Awarding Body (1998). *Handbook for the National Licensee's Certificate Off-Licence: 1998*. National Licensee's Certificate Awarding Body.

National Licensee's Certificate Awarding Body (1998). *Handbook for the National Licensee's Certificate On-Trade: 1998*. National Licensee's Certificate Awarding Body.

National Licensee's Certificate Awarding Body (1998). *Handbook for the National Licensee's Certificate Part IV Licence: 1998*. National Licensee's Certificate Awarding Body.

Peters, R. (1996). *Essential Law for Caterers*. 2nd edn. Hodder and Stoughton.

The marketing function

It's gone down hill since the new chap's taken over!
   I haven't been there but a friend recommended the food and the prices are good.
   The landlady's a real dragon – threw us out for asking for a new glass.
   It's in the *Good Beer Guide* and Egon Ronay recommends it.

It has often been stated that even the most effective marketing is spoilt by the least controllable – word of mouth – as the above quotes testify. However the managers of licensed houses require more than just personnel recommendation in order for them to maintain and grow their clientele. This process is known by the generic term 'marketing' but is interrelated to many other areas of concern to the manager. Successful marketing of an outlet depends on the product being offered (see Chapter 5), the people who operate the business (see Chapter 6) and the place itself (Chapters 2 and 3). Marketing concerns the processes of defining your customers' needs and expectations, of informing your clients of the products and services you offer and of creating a desire within those customers to visit and then visit time and time again.

It should be noted that, as a business serving the local or micro market, the range of marketing opportunities may be limited and only large chains would be able to generate the critical mass for large advertising and promotion. It should be further noted that although most licensed house managers do not possess formal marketing skills most of the techniques in this chapter can be applied with a high level of success by innovative and dynamic licensed trade managers.

The marketing environment

Any discussion of marketing must start with an understanding of the environment within which an organization exists. This environment is dynamic and, due to a range of different factors, may change at a very fast rate.

We can define the licensed retail marketing environment as the external factors which may vary over time and over which the individual organization has very little or no control. These are simply expressed as political, economic, technological and social (PETS) factors.

The *political* environment is an expression of the government of the day's policies and strategies in terms of taxation, employment law, competition law and fiscal management. These policies will determine the way in which the organization must operate within the legal framework, the action we must take in various business operations such as employment, dismissal, health, safety and hygiene or opening hours.

Both the political machinations and economic changes in the wider world will govern the *economic* environment within any particular market. In times of recession customers will seek better value for their money, and their disposable income will also be less as many customers reduce spending on luxuries. However, the effect of recession or boom will be affected by both the size of the operation and its market. If the operation merely serves those who are likely to be unaffected by difficult economic conditions the effect of recession will be less. The most important impact on the licensed house manager will be whether or not they are able to maximize opportunities in either boom or recession.

The *social* environment is the ever-changing values, expectation and desires of the population and market the organization serves. Lifestyles change from generation to generation and the new millennium will be no different. Each age group, socioeconomic grouping, each set of individuals will have their own set of expectations from licensed premises. The diverse culture within which we find ourselves must be reflected in what the organization does. This would include the different types of dishes on the menu, the range of drinks available and the facilities on offer. An ideal example of these changes and the need to cater for them can be given by the growth in the family pub. With pressurized leisure time and more affluence in the 1990s many families now wish to spend time together in a range of activities. With young children being unable to sit still for a long period, families were reluctant to eat out in restaurants and pubs other than those with beer gardens where children could run around, and so were limited by fair weather. Publicans themselves were unlikely to encourage children because of the disturbance to other customers. This left a vast untapped market for mixing the needs of parents and children. The growth in the late 1990s of Brewer's Fayre (Whitbread) and Big Steak Houses (Bass) concepts in licensed houses were developed with Charlie Chalk® and Wacky Warehouse® children's activities within the operation. Here the adults could relax and eat whilst the children played in a supervised environment.

Other sociological changes would include environmental and 'green' factors, safe environment, differentiated products, the litigation culture and the social belonging needs of the customers.

The final external influence on the organization is that of *technology*. The effect of technology is not merely in terms of the systems and processes used to deliver and control the processes and products but the wider effect on people and their lifestyles. The growths of communication media from fax to the Internet; from mobile phones to video conferencing means that we face changes in the way we work, travel and socialize. The specific effects of these changes on the market for licensed houses are not fully realized but meeting the demands of these changes requires both planning and a considered approach. The use of technology in the industry is defined further in Chapter 7.

Markets, market demand and definitions in licensed houses marketing

The marketing approaches required of the licensed house are the same as those in any enterprise. The approaches to marketing in this sector have changed in recent years; in fact it may be said that for the first time the marketing of the licensed retail venue has become more important than the product itself. However, to begin our look at marketing we must first define a series of concepts that delineate the factors to be identified in seeking to establish good marketing practice.

Markets

These define the users or potential users of any product or service. The main markets from licensed retail houses are those of provision of drink, food and, possibly, accommodation. These markets in themselves have many submarkets or segments within which organizations may flourish if they can meet the client's needs. Many of the needs of the customers are beyond the lower-level needs for food, water shelter, money or security but are those of the higher-order social, esteem and self-actualization needs (Maslow, 1949). These are concerned with the social aspect of the licensed house – a place to meet, the friendly atmosphere, relaxation or even being seen within a popular or fashionable establishment. In order that house managers meet these needs they must be aware of what the customer actually requires, how many of this type of client are within a given area or how far they are willing to travel. According to Teare *et al.* (1994) the primary segmentation variables of the hospitality industry are defined as:

- area, country or region of market origin, including nationality

- socioeconomic, demographic and tenure groups

- psychographic or lifestyle groups

- behavioural groups, including usage groups, usage rates, loyalty status and attitudes towards the product or service.

Each of these different groupings will affect the behaviour of your customers, determine where they go, what they buy, what they can afford, how often they visit and even which products they buy when they visit.

Market demand

The demand for a service or product determines whether or not any organization will be successful. It is the potential number of people who might use your establishment. If you were a public house in the middle of the country miles from any habitation on a minor road the demand for your establishment might be low. The same is potentially true even if you are in a highly populated area if there are number of similar outlets competing for your potential customers.

The demand for your product or service will vary over time dependent on a number of different factors relating to the twin drives of price and quality. Price and quality of product such as alcoholic drink and food in managed houses will be determined by company policy or economic dictats, however, quality of service and facilities will have a major role in determining demand.

Market analysis and planning

In order that a licensed house manager succeeds in marketing their unit they must first determine the needs, wants and desires of their potential customers. This involves both an investigation of the local or regional environment and the nature of any competition in that locality. Such analysis of market research will need to be monitored and adapted regularly in order to ensure that the manager responds to changes as or before they occur.

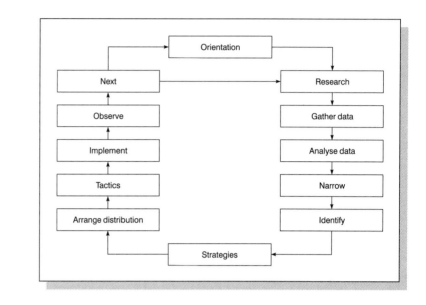

Figure 4.1
The marketing planning process
Source: After Wearne and Morrison, 1996.

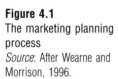

The planning process itself is a cyclical one and will involve the management in reviewing their actions at points within the cycle. The cycle given in Figure 4.1 is based on the work of Wearne and Morrison (1996) who developed the acronym ORGANISATION to demonstrate the process in action.

1 *Orientation*: the direction and purpose of the enterprise. This refers to the products and services that an operation wishes to supply to its potential consumers. This is often expressed in a mission statement but would also encompass the philosophies of the owners and management in achieving that mission. For example: 'The White Lion will provide its customers with a wide range of food and drink to meet their needs in a friendly efficient manner at a reasonable cost and within a safe and welcoming environment.'

2 *Research*: who exactly are our potential customers? What do they require? When do they require it? Do different segments require different things? We need to know everything we possibly can about our market, even though we may not be able to meet all their needs. What we do need to do is to meet enough customers' needs to become and remain profitable.

3 *Gather data*: much of the data we require will be available through national trends or other statistical sources. However, sales figures, customer and staff feedback or even questionnaires will provide even more information.

4 *Analyse data*: the process of data assessment is not necessarily complex or even reliant on statistical analysis. What we are looking for is trends and an overall picture. Once this picture

is clear we can proceed to identify which parts of the market we wish to service.

5 *Narrow*: it will be necessary to focus on the particular segments or niches within a market that we can or want to fulfil. To paraphrase Abraham Lincoln 'you can't please all of the people all of the time' is a handy *aide-mémoir* at this point. Setting realistic segments to capture will not only allow you to satisfy customers but will also allow you to concentrate both your marketing effort and your products to meet those needs.

6 *Identify*: what you are now going to do, bearing in mind your strengths and weaknesses, the market, the data you have and your mission statement. 'The engine or driving force for the entire marketing planning process' (Wearne and Morrison, 1996).

7 *Strategies*: we know where we are going, now how do we get there? We need to now set up the marketing mix we are going to employ (see from the section 'Market research' onwards). This marketing mix strategy will drive all our further actions.

8 *Arrange distribution*: putting the message in front of the customers. Where? When? How often? How much?

9 *Tactics*: determine your advertising and promotional activities. Which are we going to use? In house? Newspapers? Direct mail? (See the 'Promotion' section in this chapter.)

10 *Implement*: we have decided what we have got, we know where we are going and we believe we know how to do it. Let us launch it!

11 *Observe*: the end results need to be observed. How many new customers do we now have? Are we meeting their needs? Are sales and profits up or down? Is the cost worth it?

12 *Next*: How do we now improve our marketing effort? Examine the media, the message and the marketing mix, and examine their shortfalls and successes. Eliminate the shortfall and enhance the successes.

Such planning should lead us to a position where we have a clear idea of where we are going and how to get there. The next stage should be to carry out the research, but before that we should examine the segmentation within the markets we wish to serve in more detail.

Segmentation

There are several ways to delineate the different sectors of any market – by age, sex, location, income, and benefits sought or social class. Such segmentation may be in terms of locals and visitors, regular and infrequent, but these segments will not truly reflect the total mix of customers for most licensed outlets. A better segmentation may be in terms of business users, social users, independent travellers and occasional diners.

1 *Business users*: those clients who frequent the establishment for business meetings, lunches, dinners and after-work drinks. Mainly daytime weekday users who normally require more than just drinks. Drink-drive laws and the decline of the 'business lunch' may reduce alcohol consumption.

2 *Social users*: those utilizing the establishment for purely social purposes. May be mainly local trade or a mix of local and wider area depending on the location and products on offer. Depending on location may be more evening and weekend oriented. Both alcohol and food may be required by this group.

3 Travellers: those on a journey who stop for refreshment. May have limited alcoholic needs but will normally require food. Major users of wayside inns especially during summer periods. Main trade is in resort and tourist active areas.

This simple segmentation can be broken down further according to various behaviours and other factors:

1 *Demographic segments*: based on age. Each age may well require different products or services from the licensed retail establishment. Young and old alike may require food drink, entertainment and even accommodation, but the particular style they require is radically different. The same radical difference will be true between genders and even in life stages. For example the 'macho camaraderie' of the traditional pub may well not suit female visitors, whilst the establishment beloved by the single man would not meet the needs of the family man with three children.

2 *Social class segments*: there are two styles.
   (a) Sociodemographics, which segments people into grouping according to their age, sex, occupation, disposable income and place of origin.
   (b) Psychographic, which divides, peoples according to their lifestyle, personality traits and drives. The classic A, B, C1, C2, D and E social class bandings are not often used in good marketing but remain a useful but simplistic means of grouping people.

3 *User segments*: these can be categorized into three separate types – loyal, shifting and celebratory (Wearne and Morrison, 1996). Loyal customers are those who use a licensed house regularly and may return on a weekly, monthly or even daily

basis. Shifting customers are constantly looking for new experiences and will shift from location to location depending on moods, fashion or even weather. Celebratory segments are those who visit only when they have a specific occasion either public (Hallowe'en, New Year's Eve, etc.) or private (birthday, anniversary).

4 *Price segments*: the last distinct segment in terms of licensed houses is in pricing. The price that individuals wish to pay for the products and facilities on offer will determine which type of establishment they frequent, based on their personal financial worth and their willingness to spend it.

One final way to determine segments is given by Wearne and Morrison (1996) as 'fors, against, indifferent and unawares'. Those who already use our establishment and will continue to do so are 'fors'. Those who either because of previous experience or what we offer will not use us are 'against'. The indifferent know about our products but do not require what we have on offer. The unawares do not know of what we have on offer.

Our marketing strategy, therefore, would be to maintain or expand the custom of the fors, inform the unawares, change what we offer to attract the indifferent and even perhaps change the minds of those who are against.

Market research

To establish where these potential users are, what they want and such vital data as how much they can or would spend, we must carry out some market research. This research can be very simple and straightforward and carried out in house, or it can involve a great deal of both desk-based (secondary) or field (primary) data collection.

One of the main problems with data we collect is that it may mislead us.

Case study

A case in point

A pub and restaurant in rural South Wales received data from CAMRA showing the dramatic growth in real ale consumption and the fact that in recent years real ale production had increased over 200 per cent. The licensee, fresh from college, thought that this was for him. His market was based on local farm workers, villagers, business trade at lunchtime and evening, and social users at the weekend. Being near to population centres and the M4 meant a number of travellers would also use his establishment. In other words this was the projected market for the real ale product from the data he received. After spending a large amount of hard-earned profit on the installation of specialist equipment, the bar was relaunched. Initial trade was high but the price of the real ale put off his local users and many of the travelling customers avoided the strong ales, and a local drive against drink-driving diminished trade. The restaurant trade suffered as a consequence and after one summer the project was abandoned. Why did it fail? Mainly because the licensee saw a product he thought would fit. He did not enquire of his existing customers whether they wanted it; he had not thought through the process to the end point. Although some establishments because of their location, ambience and reputation may be able to sell a product, it does not mean every establishment can.

Thus we must not only research products but also whether or not there are enough customers to cover initial outlay and make a profit.

The outcome of our planning will be given by a series of strategies and tactics designed to ensure we inform the right people of what we have to offer and have on offer what our potential customers require – the marketing mix.

The marketing mix

The marketing mix is the interplay of six factors, which we combine in order to meet both the marketing and the organization's objectives. Many of the mix items will be expressed in terms of tactics or action designed to achieve our overall aims. These tactics should be in harmony with each other and should not send out conflicting messages to our potential users.

The six elements are

- Place: where is the place? Location!

- Product: what we will sell? How will we sell it?

- Promotion: how do we tell the customers about what we have to offer?

- Pricing: how much do we charge them for what we have?

- People: who will our customers be?

- Positioning: what sort of establishment do we wish to be perceived as?

The mix between the elements determines whether or not we will achieve a competitive advantage over others attempting to serve the same market.

Competitive advantage

In theory competitive advantage in any market can be seen as being the ability of any establishment to attract customers to their operation rather than another. This has been expressed by many strategic and marketing writers, Kotler among them, as being a prime concern of managers. 'Competitive advantage is a company's ability to perform in one or more ways that competitors will not or can not match' (Kotler, 2000). However, as Kotler states these competitive advantages are only useful where the customer actually wishes to partake of the advantage, therefore, competitive advantage is only useful where the advantage is also a customer advantage. Those operations that achieve customer advantages consistently will 'deliver high customer value and satisfaction, which leads to high repeat purchases and high company profitability' (Kotler, 2000).

In reality this means that any licensed house must offer what it is its customers need, and deliver those products and services consistently well. You may well face nearby competitors that offer a similar product or similar facilities, but success will be determined not only by the number of competitors and how good or cheap they are but by whether the customers wish to use your establishment more often. Price is not the only determinant, nor is location, nor is product or even promotion; each must fit the customers' needs when they visit you. They may visit every night or only once or twice a year for a special occasion, if you meet their needs on each occasion they will come again, if you do not they will go elsewhere!

Product and branding

Product

The product in some industries may only refer to the physical thing that a company produces but in the licensed trade, as in the rest of the hospitality industry, the product is not only the physical things we sell but also the service provided by the establishment. Therefore, when we talk about the product in terms of licensed premises, we are talking about both the food, drink and other consumables and the style of service, the customer approach, the décor, ambience and, most importantly, the people who serve the consumables. The people side is covered later in this chapter and in Chapter 6, and the details of the products and choosing them in Chapter 5. However, it is important to look further at the ways in which the product should be designed and the marketing emphasis upon it.

If possible the product you sell should be uniquely yours, something that others may wish to have but do not, something that the customer obviously requires but also something that separates you from your competitors, a unique selling point (USP). This USP should be something that your customers both enjoy and feel that they are part of. Your regulars should love it as a place to relax and enjoy themselves, your new trade should be excited by it, want to join in, want to come again. Wearne and Morrison (1996) define this as 'always aim to create for customers a sense of ownership or belonging to an establishment'.

This is an extremely difficult point to achieve in the modern competitive environment. In towns and cities, or even in large villages, there will be several other companies or operators competing for the same business. Each establishment will attempt to create an individual product with which to achieve that end. It has become even more difficult in recent years with the proliferation of branded products being produced by many large companies.

Branding

A brand is a product or service that has its own image, personality and style. The consumer will, through promotion or public relations (PR), associate differing brands with differing lifestyles, places and social level. The more complete the brand image the more closely customer will identify with it. The two types of branding within the licensed trade industry are the unit brand and the product brand.

The unit brand ● ● ●

The Whitbread brand, Beefeater, for example is synonymous with steak and fries, a friendly atmosphere, reasonably priced with many special offers, and a basic product that does not vary from unit to unit. This means that wherever you go in Britain the Beefeater nearest to you will have the same basic menu, range of products and promotion, and staff in similar uniforms. The only variation comes in the local theme of the décor, although there is a great deal of similarity between many of the units. Many other companies have developed similar brands in the licensed trade industry, e.g., Mulligans, Tut 'n Shive, Firkin Pubs, Weather-spoons, Brewers Fayre, Old Orleans and Big Steak Houses.

The strength of the branding by larger companies lies in the consistency of product and the power of promotion. It allows companies to brand their units on a national basis, using national newspapers, television and radio to push the image. It does mean, however, that the management of such houses relies on maintaining the set standards and if one unit suffers bad publicity others in the same chain may also suffer.

Case study

Another case in point

In 1999 a pub and restaurant in Cardiff, part of a branded chain, was investigated by BBC Wales current affairs programme *Week In Week Out*. The investigation stemmed from a complaint by an ex-member of staff to the programme about food safety practices at the restaurant. An undercover film crew recorded a number of serious incidents in contravention of the Food Safety Act 1990 condoned by local management. When it was screened the effect on the house was immediate with a serious drop in business, but three other brand restaurants in the area also lost trade, 'if they do it there they'll do it elsewhere too'. The practices at the restaurant were strictly against all company policy and practice, and the company launched an immediate investigation. The management of the restaurant were disciplined and new management brought in. All other restaurants in the chain were cleared of any wrongdoing of this nature but 'the mud still sticks'. A year on from that incident many local people are wary of the brand and the original restaurant still has to reach its preinvestigation level of business.

Product brands

The products within the licensed field are among the strongest brands in marketing. Their image is reinforced via innovative media promotion, sponsorship and PR. The brands are mainly those associated with beer, spirits, liqueurs and soft drinks but may also apply to other consumables. The success of branding lies very heavily on the promotion process, which is used to 'modify the perception of the customer of the product and their experience of it' (Teare *et al.*, 1994) This promotional activity needs constant attention if the product is to maintain its competitive edge. Product development is one means of keeping products in the public eye and launching promotions upon the premise of being new and improved. However, with most drink products such innovation may have disastrous outcomes, e.g., the attempted launch of new Coca-Cola© in the 1970s. The drinkers of the product greeted this new and 'improved' product with derision and the company quickly reverted to the old recipe. Variations on product in the beverage market do work where the original is also retained and the new product is in some way different, e.g., diet versions of soft drinks, premium versions of lagers or lite versions of Alco-pops.

Product life cycle

As discussed in Chapter 5 all products have life cycles that are both physical and image based. A product may last as long as Vino Santo, a style and method of wine-making noted by the ancient Greeks, or *uisge beathe* the Gaelic term for whisky, probably first distilled in Ireland in the fifteenth century. On the other hand the product life cycle may be as brief as those of many of the ready-to-drink (RDT) bottled beverages or alcopops that are introduced at the beginning of each season – summer, Christmas, etc. – and have been withdrawn before that season ends. For example, alcoholic water had a remarkably short life span of a couple of months when introduced in 1996. Many hundreds of new products are introduced to the consumer each year. The majority of these fail or do not fully reach the target market they were designed for, the 'dogs', others become the 'plough horses' and a few become 'stars'. Analysis of the turnover of the product will help the licensee, and prevent overstocking of a range that has reached the end of its viable life cycle.

Promotion

Promotion is the process of ensuring that your customers know about your products and services, and its aim is to encourage them to sample these by appealing to their needs or desires. The process of communication can be one of two different types normally defined as direct and indirect.

Direct	Indirect
Personal selling	Advertising
Direct mail	Brochures
Sales promotion	Publicity
Product presentation	Signs and displays
Point of sale activity	
Source: Wearne and Morrison, 1996.	

Table 4.1
Process communication types

Personal selling in licensed houses tends to be by service staff and is key in achieving customer satisfaction. The other direct promotion activities are all used to some extent by licensed house managers, each has potential advantages and drawbacks but by mixing them one may assist even the smallest outlet to improve its sales.

Direct mail

Not normally used by tied or free houses or even by individual managers of managed units, this type of promotion is expensive and must be carefully monitored in its effectiveness. Sending details of new menus when opening a new establishment or when relaunching the unit in a different guise may be solid reasons for using direct mail but, unlike hotels which keep an extensive guest history, we may not actually know the addresses of our customers. So mailshots in the locality either by using agencies to deliver the leaflets or flyers or delivering them ourselves are probably the best use of mailing.

Brochures

Again these are not used to any great extent particularly in owner-operator pubs but if the unit has a range of facilities on offer (conference, wedding, skittles, etc.) then it may be useful to print a brochure stating both details of the facilities and/or prices. Large chain establishments will use brochures often in the form of maps showing where all their branches are and giving details of the chain as a whole.

Sales promotion

Sales promotion is the process of short-term drives to attract customers. They are designed to 'solve a business problem or exploit a market opportunity' (Wearne and Morrison, 1996).

The range of possible promotions is vast and, although repeatable, should be used only to address particular problem areas. These could involve annual events, food or liquor events, openings, parties or special value days. Table 4.2 shows a small selection of possible events and the type of promotions that could be run.

Product presentation and point-of-sale activity

The possible range of products available in licensed houses is immense and careful decisions have to be made on the way in which the products are presented to the customer. On the food

Title	Theme	Special arrangements
St Valentine's day	Love and lovers; hearts and romance	Hearts and cupids decoration. Staff wearing red hearts. Lovers' cocktails. Candlelight meals in the restaurant. Romantic music/disco. Discounts for couples
St Patrick's day	The shamrock and the green	Green decorations. Shamrocks for all customers. Promotion in Irish drinks (Guinness, Jamesons, Bailey's, etc.). Obviously theme night for Irish theme pubs. Dublin Bay prawns, Guinness pie, or Irish stew
Charity events	Fund-raising and public relations	Use of celebrity to attract participation Coverage by media. Either wacky events (sponsored bed-push, custard-pie fight, etc.) or sporting or quiz nights. Pile-of-pennies events are passé
World cup	Sports fans to the fore.	Large-screen televisions. World cup theme promotions and posters. Staff in national kit. Signs showing the draw and the progression of your team. Half-time promotions

Table 4.2 Examples of promotional activities

side the menu or display boards are a simple way of presenting the wares for sale. Attractive salad bars and cold buffets are all very good ways of presenting the food but the innovative display of the raw food in chilled cabinets with the chef cooking the customer's choice in plain view may be even better.

With bottled products displays behind the bar must attract the customers eye, particularly to those products the establishments wishes to sell as part of a product promotion. Bottles or optics are designed to show the customer that they are there and are normally free from the maker or the wholesaler. Bottle stacks are eye-catching especially when large and well lit. Babys, mixers and other bottles can be displayed on ordinary shelving at eye level with the main stock below in refrigerators. If the refrigerators are mounted at eye level their appeal may be enhanced. The important point is that the consumer can see the products and pick out their favourites from the crowd. Innovative or eye-catching labels on display will attract consumers to new products.

Draught beers are normally presented through the beer engines or founts. The badged handles to real ale engines are a means of advertising the beer on sale and the range that the establishment has on offer. Many draught-beer display boxes on the bar are also lit to attract the eye.

At the point of sale, i.e., the bar or restaurant, the manager of the business may find it useful not just to draw customers' attention to their immediate purchase but also to subsidiary or later purchases. Examples in this area would include prominent displays of crisp products or cigars at the bar and dessert or coffee menus on the table. Although you may not sell on that occasion, perhaps the next time the customer comes to the bar or after they finish their meal they will order subsidiary items.

Signs and displays

When many industries and companies are using increasingly more technologically driven signs and notices it is interesting to note that more signs in public houses and other licensed premises are on chalkboards – not necessarily written in chalk, which fades and is dusty, but in wax pen designed to look like chalk. This type of display is extremely effective in situations where the house offers a changing range of products particularly in the food area. There is ample opportunity for the use of colour and design on the board, both key issues in any display and signage.

Displays of menus and other materials or events should be sited at key points in the licensed house. The points of entry, behind or on the bar and at the entrance to the restaurant are all key areas.

Advertising

Advertising is one of the licensed house's main means of spreading the word about itself. Advertising is not just using media such as television or newspaper to get that message across but is a range of allied activities including external signage, leaflets, tent cards and signature items bearing the logo or name of the outlet (matches, pens, cocktail stirrers, etc.). According to Wearne and Morrison (1996) there are four types of advertisements; reach, teach, preach and reminder:

1 *Reach*: the selling of a promotion via a variety of forms. This could include newspaper adverts, banner across the front of the premises or brochures within the establishment. The aim is to generate immediate action by the customer. Pricing is one of the main subjects of such advertising. It will be used to bring to the customer's attention special events, new products or changes to the premises themselves.

2 *Teach*: to tell a specific segment of the market about the benefits of using the establishment and generate responses in the medium term. Prices are rarely mentioned.

3 *Preach*: the creation of an image of the establishment in the potential customer's mind and creating a desire to visit the establishment the next time they are looking to visit your type of establishment. Price is rarely an issue but the USPs of the house should be to the fore.

4 *Reminder*: this is simply keeping your establishment in front of the customer. The important effort here is frequent repeats of the message so that you constantly remind the customer where you are. Signature items are one means of achieving this, but regular media adverts may be more effective.

Advertising levels

Advertising in the licensed trade industry occurs at three levels: product, company and unit. Each has its own concerns and advertising needs.

Product advertising • • •

Only a relatively small amount of the industry sells its own alcoholic products and these are mainly small-scale micro-breweries. The rest of the industry sells branded products known locally or nationally. The national brands have an extremely high profile approach to media-based advertising.

Many of the award-winning television and newspaper adverts of recent years have been coined by alcohol brands. The use,

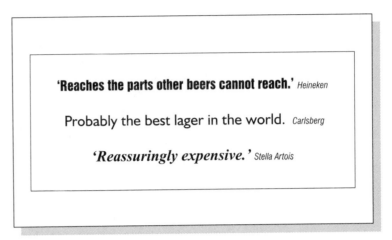

Figure 4.2
Catch phrases used in the promotion of alcoholic beverages

particularly, of humour has been the key to these adverts (see Figure 4.2) and although mainly reach and preach in their emphasis they have also served as the means of keeping the products name on everyone's lips.

Recently the Portman Group guidelines (see Chapter 8) on the advertisements for alcohol-based products has meant that future adverts would not be based on sexual attraction or mass or binge drinking.

Further product advertising is summarized in Table 4.3.

Type	Purpose
Sponsorship	Mainly to keep the name of the company in the public eye. The sponsorship of cups, of teams or tours especially when linked to television and media coverage, ensures a very positive image for the product. Unfortunately bad publicity from these events may detract from the products image
Bar paraphernalia	Bar towels, ice buckets, coasters, beer mats, drip trays, ashtrays, umbrellas and glasses ensure the customers are reminded of the product
Outdoor advertising	The use of billboard advertising will reinforce the message put out via other media and may reach, preach and remind customers of the product

Table 4.3
Illustrations of product advertising

Company and brands · · ·

The larger companies will spend considerable time and money advertising their branded houses and restaurants. This advertising is more prominent in the large pub restaurant chains, e.g., Beefeater, Harvester and Big Steak. In advertising for these brands the companies wish to 'preach' about the characteristics of the brands. The use of television is less important than newspapers (both local and national), brochures and direct mail. Smaller chains of houses will use local media to advertise their brands.

Unit advertisements · · ·

Most establishments in the licensed trade industry will rely on advertising at unit level to reach, preach and remind their customers. Special events may be the most prolific use of advertising but many larger units may wish to advertise regularly especially if they have a large food element in their operation.

Advertising is potentially a positive force for attracting customers but before launching an aspect of advertising the licensed house manager must consider the following:

1 The communication within the advertisement should always be such that the customer can differentiate your advert from others offering similar products or services.

2 Advertising does not solve all problems, 'it is not a panacea for poor marketing in other areas of the marketing mix' (Wearne and Morrison, 1996)

3 Skill and technical know-how are key in producing good advertising. The providers of the media itself may be able to offer help in this area, but if any major effort is to be launched then an advertising agency may be a much better bet.

4 The process of advertising is expensive; assess the benefit of any advertising effort and review both the media and the message each time it is used.

5 Evaluation of promotional methods: which is the best for you? Which can you afford? Which will have the maximum effect and which the least? Will you alienate old customers or enhance their experience too?

Pricing

The price for a product or service has several facets, first, a purely accounting one and, second, a marketing one. The accounting facet is concerned with meeting the costs of the operation and obtaining a profit margin. The costs of the operation are those concerned with not only the operation of the business but also the setting-up costs. Thus as well as meeting the variable costs of the drink or food, electricity, gas, washing, cleaning, etc., the prices charged must also cover the fixed costs such as staff costs, rates, loan repayments, mortgages, or rent, etc., and include VAT. The profit level is obviously important to the manager or owner, as this is either their measure of success or their livelihood. Profit levels must also be able to cover planned capital expenditure into the future. Thus for simplicity the price of the product would be a function of PRICE = Cost of sales (food or drink) + Contribution to operating costs + Contribution to fixed costs + profit required.

The prices charged by an establishment are normally set according to what the target market for the operation will bear. As there are many market sectors there will also be a number of different pricing strategies. In licensed premises it is often the pricing that determines the type of clientele the operation has, particularly when the product and service match the prices. Customers paying a premium price for the products would expect high-quality products, service and furnishings but also other unique points such as décor, ambience or entertainment. However, such a premium pricing strategy may limit the size of the market or use of the operation for special occasions only.

The main concern for licensed house managers is that the prices of their products and services are perceived by the customers as being value for money no matter what those prices are. If the consumer believes that they are overpaying for what they receive they will not use the establishment again. However, if they believe that they have received excellent value for money, not only will they return but they will also come again and again. This in itself may cause problems for the manager as being too popular brings congestion, overstressed staff and systems and, possibly, unhappy customers. Thus a balance has to be sought by the manager to enable trade to remain high whilst ensuring that customer satisfaction also remains high.

Pricing can also be important as a promotional tool in attracting customers into the establishment at normally quiet times. The use of 'happy hours', early-bird menus, special lunch offers or discounts to particular groups of users (e.g., students or the over 50s) are prime examples of this. This strategy serves a number of purposes. First, it brings in customers who would not use the establishment or it moves them to off peak times. Second, it means that the fixed costs of the operation, staff costs, capital recovery and the variable costs of staying open are being met even if the profit margins are lower. Third, it may actually increase overall custom as those who come for the lower price times and events either stay on past the event or purchase higher margin products as well as the lower margin ones. This final type of effect can be applied to food within the operation but is not normally applied to the liquor. It is termed the 'loss leader'. This, for example, will be a product that is priced at a low profit margin or even breakeven and is intended to attract customers to higher margin products. A prime example of this occurs in steak restaurants. The steaks themselves (with vegetables) are priced very competitively or even discounted below the cost price, however, the customer would then be sold the starters, desserts, wines, liqueurs or coffees on offer, by skilled sales staff, at higher margins.

This lowering of prices is also associated with new premises, or following refurbishment, to attract new clientele in many cases away from other operations. This market penetration pricing strategy will also be used to launch a new product or service within the establishment.

Place

The location of the licensed establishment has always been one of the most important aspects of success. No matter how competitive the pricing, how wonderful the décor or how much you spend on promotion it will be difficult to overcome a disadvantageous position. The only recognized way of doing it is in fact to offer a product that nobody else has, which will attract the consumers to wherever you are. This, though, in the modern licensed market house has become almost impossible as the range of competitors is such that difficulties of travel, especially in view of drink-drive laws, means a substitution to nearer establishments may be often preferred.

As noted in Table 4.4, prime locations for licensed premises are a function of their target markets. Rural pubs in isolated villages are sole providers and their location ensures a base level of trade throughout the year, but unless the region also has a tourist trade in the summer the local market is all it may have. Picturesque village pubs near urban areas or in tourist areas may attract both the local and visiting trade but with other villages in the area it may take specialized products or services to attract the customers to their quaint little tavern. One has only to visit Cotswold village pubs in England to perceive how this may work.

People

This applies to two particular types of people: those who will frequent your establishment and those who will be your employees.

Customers

The choice in terms of customers has been discussed in the 'Segmentation' section of this chapter, however, it requires a clear understanding of what your market is if you are to successfully market to these customers.

Location	Advantages	Disadvantages
Urban centres	1 High passing trade 2 Concentration of entertainment in the area especially at weekends 3 Co-operation with other landlords especially on security (see Chapter 8) 4 Benefits during peak shopping times, e.g., Christmas	1 High competition 2 High peaks and low troughs of trade 3 Higher incidence of drink-related violence 4 Small local trade
Student residential areas	1 High volume, value seeking customers 2 May purchase a range of related products, food, music, pool, etc. 3 Simple promotional activities, i.e., drink related 4 Would allow for 'locals' trade in separate bar	1 High volume in term time only 2 Trade may diminish as term progresses 3 May be attracted to trendier operation 4 Requires services beyond drink (see 2 in Advantages column)
Office districts	1 High trade in lunchtime and early evening 2 Customers are both food and drink oriented 3 High affluence 4 Entertaining of clients thus expansion of trade	1 Very low trade or nonexistent in late evening and weekends 2 Consumer loyalty low and movement likely
Industrial estates	As above, plus: 5 Likely competition may only be non-alcohol related or even non-existent	1 Very low trade or nonexistent in late evening and weekends 2 Reliance on cars from work may reduce intake levels of alcohol
Tourist venue	1 High levels of trade 2 Range of consumers, therefore wide range of selling possible 3 Affluence or willingness to spend may be high	1 May be seasonal in nature 2 Reliant on the weather 3 May have very small local trade 4 High travel distance
Residential areas	1 Local and fixed population to draw upon 2 Targeting of customers and their expectations easy based on the type of housing 3 Products, services and pricing tailored to meet predictable clientele 4 Low travel distance	1 Only marginal chances for expansion of trade 2 May undergo user fatigue unless minor changes occur 3 May be sensitive to price, product or service changes

Table 4.4 The relationship between location and target markets

According to Wearne and Morrison (1996) there are three different people strategies we may adopt:

- *undifferentiated* – mass marketing
- *differentiated* – selective markets
- *concentrated* – specialized markets.

The mass marketing approach epitomized by Henry Ford and the model T is no longer a valid strategy as, even in most basic of commodities, there is sufficient competition to force companies to market to selected sectors. It is even more invalid in the licensed house sector where, although units may cater for a wide range of customers, they cannot satisfy all possible people sectors.

Differentiated marketing is where the marketing effort is aimed at specific sector/s. These may be fairly wide or cover several sectors. This is the main type of people approach within the licensed house marketing sector – meeting the needs of similar sectors rather than a generic or specialized one. Specialized license houses will exist but both their client base and number is small. Such specialization tends to rely purely on the establishment being fashionable, however, once a newer even more chic place opens, the clients may move.

Employees

It is an often missed element of the marketing mix that the people actually selling your product for you also have a key role in the successful marketing of an establishment. Their customer approach, communication and dexterity will all determine whether or not your customers have their expectations met. The process of attracting, developing and retaining employees is dealt with in more detail in Chapter 6.

The overall marketing strategy

The overall marketing strategy for a licensed house manager, no matter from which subsector, will be to maximize the number of customers they have. It order to do so they must ensure that they have targeted the customers they believe they will have, and in targeting them have found out what it is they require. The next stage is to ensure that the rest of the marketing mix, the product, people, pricing, placement and promotion, is in place to meet the market's requirements. The design and implementation of unique selling points and competitive advantages are key in achieving successful marketing. Marketing, however, is not a panacea in itself. It must be used in conjunction with the physical design of premises, the human resources of the organization and the products and styles of service to meet customers expectations and needs.

Summary propositions

1 The marketing environment of any establishment is key to all other marketing decisions.

2 An understanding of market segments and potential customer types is important in designing a marketing mix.

3 Market research can provide detailed clues as to how to construct your marketing mix.

4 The marketing mix of product, promotion, pricing, people and place requires a systematic and holistic approach in order to achieve success.

Summary questions

1 Identify a local hostelry. What external influences affect the way in which the hostelry operates? How would changes in the economic, political, social or technological environments affect that hostelry?

2 You as the manager of a city-centre pub want to find out whether or not you offer what city-centre users want. Which research methods would you use in order to determine this information?

3 Customers' comments have recently centred on a tired image for the products on sale in your public house. What steps would you take to remedy this image?

4 Business in your wine bar is steady but not impressive. You decide you need to inform more people in the local area of your products and services. How would you go about this?

Case study

'Just lucky I guess.' Kim Barrette was recently in the final of the Best Pub in Britain competition, a tremendous achievement as the pub had only been open for 2 years. Kim and a partner had converted a large farmhouse and barn on the outskirts of Exeter into a pub-restaurant complex whilst around them a housing estate of three- and four-bedroom houses had been built up. The old farmhouse still backed on to farmland and was close to the A38 main road, and the Meadowfield estate now housed over 3000 people. The Chequers, named after the original farm, has a 95 seat restaurant which has a justifiable reputation as having a good value high-quality menu. It specializes in a seafood menu from the local seaports with a vast range of home-made sweets.

The quote above is from the start of an interview with *Hospitality Marketing* magazine on the secrets of the Chequers's success. Kim continued 'I don't have a marketing strategy at all. I just thought that this place looked like a good conversion property and with the housing estate going up it looked to have a built-in clientele.' 'Why convert?' said the interviewer. 'Surely it would have been cheaper to build from scratch?' 'No' said Kim. 'It wasn't cost that drove the decision, it was the feel of the place. It had character already and a history dating back to the civil war! I just felt everything felt good, a new estate, an old building! We thought fish because of the local seaports, desserts because of the lack of home-made desserts in other pubs round here and I suppose its just caught on. Sometimes we make mistakes but I listen to my customers, I respond to their comments and they just seem to like it.' 'What would you say your strengths are?" Kim was asked. 'Well, I've a terrific staff, most of whom have been with me since the start. We all love serving our customers and we know most of them by name. We regularly advertise in the local papers when we have events on, and have theme events and celebrity nights quite often. We had that chap from *Eastenders* in just last week to help start the sponsored bedpush to London.'

'What weaknesses do we have? Well, it's quiet in the lunchtimes on Monday and Tuesday and between 3 p.m. and 6 p.m. most days. I don't want to push it but I just can't seem to get people in!'

1 How do you react to Kim's statement that the Chequers does it all by luck not marketing? What marketing does the Chequers do?

2 What advice would you give to Kim in completing a strategy for marketing at the pub?

3 How would you deal with the quiet times at the Chequers?

Further reading and references

Buttle, F. (1994). *Hotel and Food Service Marketing*. Holt, Rinehart and Winston.

Kotler, P. (2000). *Marketing Management*. Millenium edn. Prentice Hall.

Maslow, A. (1949). A Theory of Human Motivation. *Psychological Review*, p. 50.

Teare, R., Mazanec, J., Crawford-Welch , S. and Calver, S. (1994). *Marketing in Hospitality and Tourism*. Cassell.

Wearne, N. and Morrison, A. (1996). *Hospitality Marketing*. Butterworth-Heinemann.

Management of the products and services

Consumer profile

According to Mintel Marketing Intelligence (1996), the four most frequently cited reasons for going to a pub are:

- local/within walking distance

- pleasant landlord/bar staff [*sic*]

- good atmosphere/ambience

- my type of people go there.

This applies to all types of people and social groups; below these four however different socioeconomic groups vary in their next set of priorities. Mid-age groups (35–44) place a pleasant landlord/bar staff [*sic*] higher than other age groups. Families with children, unsurprisingly, consider 'catering for children' and 'beer gardens' important. People aged under 24 place a high emphasis on 'my kind of people' and 'games'. Category ABs give priority to 'lunchtime food' and a 'wide range of food'.

When trying to establish the customer profile and their expectations, a prospective licensed house manager should always consult the most up-to-date version of authoritative statistical sources. These include such sources as, Mintel, Key Note Reports (i.e., *UK Beer Market Feb. '99*, or *Breweries and the Beer Market May '99*), *Drink Forecast*, and local demographic reports such as those of ACORN (a geodemographic segmentation method based on the national census, which classifies consumers according to the type of residential area in which they live). However, this merely gives the theoretical side, and while it is extremely important and relevant, there is no substitute for personal research into what is actually happening at the proposed site and within the local neighbourhood. (See Chapter 4 for more information on this.)

Each venue is likely to have more than one type of customer: for instance, a pub in a city centre may have working people who pop in for lunch, as well as those who have come into town to go shopping. It is also likely that the customer mix will differ between the lunchtime and evening trade, weekday and weekend trade, and daily and seasonally. Prospective licensed house managers must be aware of these patterns, ensure that the differing groups interact sympathetically, or find methods of discouraging whichever group is least harmonious and least profitable. The loud contemporary music preferred by the under 24s is generally loathed by the grey market, especially at the volume preferred by the younger age group. Both groups live on fixed budgets (although fixed at differing levels), and so are strongly attracted by the value for money aspect of a venue. It may be that an establishment can act both as a lunchtime destination venue for the grey market and then, by removing some seating and changing the music, become a local/destination venue for the under 24s in the evening. If one group is very small it may be best to tailor the venue exclusively for the much larger group or seek a new additional type of customer, or both.

Beverage 'fit' to establishment

Having established that different establishments have different types of customers who have differing wants and expectations, the successful licensed house manager has to try to meet these expectations. It is more complex than saying that a local pub sells beer, a café bar sells wine and a nightclub sells ready-to-drink bottled beverages. As previously noted, a local, with an affluent up-market clientele, may well have a strong food trade, and so sell a high proportion of wine and spirits. Then again, a CAMRA pub may sell very little other than beer but have many different types of beer. To be able to decide what products are to be sold, the prospective licensed house manager needs to have a good understanding of the demands of the prospective clientele, and what mix of beverages in what quality–price relationship would best meet those expectations.

There are many specialist publications that describe beers, spirits and wines in great technical detail. It is not the intention of this book to repeat material that can readily be found elsewhere but rather to introduce the reader to the different types of beverages available in each category. When a decision has been reached about the actual establishment that the prospective licensed house manager would like to run, further research should be made into the current brands or individual beverages available from the relevant specialist source. These include writers such as Roger Protz and Michael Jackson (beer) or Hugh Johnson and Jancis Robinson (wine), specialist journals (such as *The Publican*), statistical reports (such as the *Drink Forecast*), professional associations (such as CAMRA) and potential suppliers.

Deciding upon beers

There has been a significant decline in beer consumption in the UK, from 65.36 million hectolitres in 1988 to 58.84 million hectolitres in 1998, However, this downward trend now appears to have bottomed out, and predictions for total beer consumption to 2003 (58.90 million hectolitres) look to remain fairly stable (*Drink Forecast*, 2000, vol. 19, no. 3). What has changed though, and is likely to continue to change, is the type of beer, ale or lager consumed and the venue in which it is consumed.

In almost all establishments where alcohol is sold, beer is sold in one form or another. Only true wine bars, with restricted licences, are likely to sell just the one kind of alcoholic beverage. Most establishments will sell a mixture of different types of beer, the main categories of which are draught and bottled.

Draught ● ● ●

It is generally accepted that there two kinds of draught beer: those that are cask conditioned and those that are 'keg' or brewery conditioned. A cask-conditioned ale is one where the beer or ale undergoes a secondary fermentation inside the cask, so that when it arrives at the pub the yeast will still be alive, and the ale, after its journey, will be cloudy and need several hours to settle. Once opened, like wine, the ale needs to be consumed within a couple of days, although some ales may have a slightly longer shelf life than others. A keg, whether it contains lager or beer, means that the contents have been conditioned in a tank at the brewery, and then filtered and pasteurized. This means that the beer will have a much longer life, but slightly less flavour, than cask ale once the barrel has been opened. However, it also means that the beverage needs to be artificially carbonated either with carbon dioxide or a carbon dioxide and nitrogen mix. Traditionally all draught beers and lagers were brewed in the UK, but it is now becoming possible to purchase some authentic European draught beers, particularly lagers. These are most popular where the customer base is slightly more sophisticated and has an above average income.

Bottled beers ● ● ●

Bottled beers range from the traditional bottled bitters, such as IPA, porter or brown ale, to the premium or designer beers, such as San Miguel. Originally, bottled beers were merely a method of enabling draught beer to be transported long distances successfully. For instance, IPA was a bottled bitter (bitter in bottle form becoming a light or pale ale) that was created to be sent out to troops in India so that they could have something to drink which resembled their normal beverage back home, hence India Pale Ale (IPA). In modern times this trend has reversed itself, so that while standard lagers could be brewed under licence in the UK for UK consumption, i.e., Foster's or Heineken, premium lagers would be made and bottled in their place of origin and then shipped to the UK. A perception was therefore created that the 'best' lagers came from outside the UK and in bottle form, e.g., Budweiser Budvar or Amstel. (With the increase in purchasing in the off-trade for home consumption, more and more beers, including real ales, are now available in bottles.) The advantage that the bottle has over the cask or keg is that the container is only opened when the customer asks for the product, so there is little wastage. Therefore, many pubs that specialize in draught beers would also have a selection, in bottle form, of the less popular beers, so that they can meet their customers' demands, however infrequently those beers are requested. In those establishments where there is little demand for beer, or at the cutting edge of fashion where drink brands change very quickly, a wide range of bottled beers may be more suitable for the clientele, than a wide range of draft beers.

The type of venue and type of customer will have a significant effect upon the type of beer sold and, as previously noted, not all venues that sell beer sell draught beer. For instance, a cocktail bar may easily be a destination venue where the clientele would feel uncomfortable holding a pint glass, but be very happy to hold a premium bottled product. Most establishments, however, have both draught and bottled beers. If the establishment is a 'real ale' pub, then a likely combination would be as many cask ales as the throughput justifies – between three and ten – and two draught lagers, one standard, such as Foster's, or Carling Black Label, and one premium, such as Budweiser or Carling Premier. The pub may also stock some very traditional British bottled beers, such as an IPA, and a stout. As the venue moves along the spectrum, away from being a real ale pub, perhaps into a more conventional local, the number of cask-conditioned ales will drop to one or none, and the number of keg bitters will rise, again to as many as are justified by demand. If the house is tied to a brewery the licensed house manager will have little choice in the beer sold, but along with the lagers, the establishment is likely to sell at least one stout style, Guinness or Caffrey's for instance, and a selection of standard and premium bitters.

As the venue moves away from the pub end of the spectrum and towards the destination venue (currently), the percentage of draught beer and lager sold will reduce in favour of premium bottled beers, probably from all around the world. If the venue is a nightclub, it is likely that there will be very little demand for draught beers – customers having learnt to dance bottle in hand (if permitted) and with the thumb over the top to prevent the drink being 'spiked'. The brand and image, the cachet, of the drink now becomes important, if everyone else can see what is being drunk. Venues are also likely to find that they have seasonal, and day to evening, weekday to weekend variations. Establishments with beer gardens, for instance, will find that on a hot sunny day, long cold lager brands such as Foster's or Heinekan will be sold, whereas on a cold winters night, a more mellow bitter or spirits will be more popular. The amount of draught beer sold will obviously affect the sizes of the barrels purchased, and this will affect the amount of storage space required. Standard barrel sizes range from the 9-gallon Firkin to the 18-gallon Kilderkin to the full 36-gallon barrel or keg. Eleven-gallon and 22-gallon barrels are also available, but are not so common. Many establishments have more than one barrel size to accommodate specific demand.

In establishments that sell draught beer, either the pumps have to be metered, to enable a full half a pint or pint to be drawn, or the glasses used have to be stamped. Whether the glass is a full pint to the top, or whether the measure is marked just below the top usually depends upon the customers. Do they see themselves as being short-changed if the beer does not come to the top or the glass, or do they prefer a full pint to the measuring line with the head above that? From the prospective licensed house manager's point of view it is more economical if their customers prefer the former glass. Obviously the landlord has to go with their customers' preference. There is research available as to regional preferences from sources such as Mintel.

In the UK there are normally only a few standard types of glasses for serving bottled beers (or ciders) in, Worthington (beers) or Pilsner (lagers) glasses perhaps. In continental Europe it is much more common for each type of beer sold to be served in its own specialist glass. The lack of specialist glasses may also account for the growing preference of younger consumers to drink directly from the bottle. Most mature consumers prefer to drink bottled beers from a glass, especially if sitting down for a meal.

Cider

The cider and perry market is much smaller than the UK beer market; consumption in 1988 was 3.10 million hectolitres but, unlike beer, this rose to 5.55 million hectolitres in 1998, and is forecast to go on rising in the near future (*Drink Forecast*, 2000). Although most cider is consumed at home, most on-trade establishments will sell at least one type of cider, although not all will have a perry. As with beer, draught and bottled versions are available, and bottled ciders range from standard versions such as Gaymer's Olde English or Strongbow, to premium brands such as Diamond White and Red Rock. The decisions on which style, and how many varieties, of cider should be carried by an individual establishment are much the same as for any other product, i.e., what is the consumer demand? It is worth noting that just as the manufacturers of RTDs are developing their product to try and ensure that young people enter the spirit-drinking market, so cider manufacturers are also developing their range with products like Kopparbergs Apple and Cranberry Cider, to develop their market.

Deciding upon spirits

Certain spirits are standard in all establishments, where spirits such as gin, whisky, brandy, vodka and rum (probably Bacardi) are sold. There is a vast range of other spirits and liqueurs that can be stocked, but this will depend upon the type of establishment and customer demand. Generally, a simple pub would have one house brand and one premium version of each main type of spirit; for instance, they may have a Courvoisier as the house brand, and Hine Antique as the premium cognac, Cossack vodka as the house brand and Absolut vodka as the premium brand, as well as other spirits if there is the demand. It is also generally true that the profit margin is much greater on the house spirits than the premium brands, and therefore this is the brand that staff should be recommended to offer if no preference is stated. (see 'Spirits and liqueurs' section for further details).

With some types of spirits it is slightly more complex to cover the full range. The house whisky is usually a blend, such as Bell's or Teacher's, and a single malt such as Glenfiddich or Glenmorangie would cover the role of premium brand. However, if that particular establishment had a strong Irish or American customer base, an Irish whiskey, such as Jameson's or a bourbon, such as Jim Beam, might be a more popular premium brand, or it may be necessary for the establishment to stock examples of all four beverages. An Irish theme pub might only stock Irish whiskeys. An establishment may also specialize in a particular type of spirit, such as whisky, as many Scottish pubs do, particularly those on a 'malt whisky' route.

At the more affluent end of the market some establishments may specialize in designer spirits, mixed drinks and cocktails. This type of establishments would include destination venues such as the Atlantic Bar and Grill in London, or Cuba in Cardiff. They have a very wide range of premium spirits, both as the basis for cocktails, but also as fashion drinks in their own right, various gins, vodkas, light and golden rums, tequilas and mescals for instance. Other establishments, such as those in the All-Bar-One or Slug and Lettuce-style bar chains, would have the basic house plus premium spirits, plus a small number of additional spirits or liqueurs such as Archer's Peach Liqueur or Baileys, as required by their customers, since in some of these establishments 50 per cent of wet sales may be from beer products.

Total sales of spirits are in decline, and have been for some years (Mintel; *Drink Forecast*, 2000). Reasons for this include the switch to increased wine drinking, which is seen as healthier, the higher alcohol levels of spirits, which cause problems with drinking and driving, and the perception among younger drinkers that some spirits, especially the dark ones, such as whisky and brandy, are old-fashioned. White spirits, gin and especially vodka are seen as more fashionable and sales are on the increase. They also make more suitable bases for modern dairy- or fruit-based cocktails. The fashion among the affluent and style conscious for cigar smoking and cigar clubs now appears to have stabilized, with few new dedicated clubs opening, but few closures of existing premises. This habit is likely to reduce the decline at the top end of the dark spirit market as premium cognacs and armagnacs are seen as a better match for cigars than the white spirits.

The general downward trend is very worrying to the spirit manufacturing market, and is one of the reasons that explains the sudden and rapid expansion of the RTD market aimed at introducing the young (24–35) market to spirits, thereby rejuvenating an ageing consumer profile, especially in the house and dark spirit markets.

Deciding upon alcoholic carbonates and RTDs

Alcoholic carbonates are drinks such as Two Dogs or Hoopers Hooch, better known colloquially as alcopops. The RTD market was developed on the back of this craze, for reasons outlined in the previous section.

The original alcopop was Two Dogs, developed in Australia in 1994 by Duncan MacGillivray (now owned by Merrydown) after an excessively large lemon harvest, when the excess was fermented into an alcoholic beverage and placed on the market to see what would happen. The immediate popularity of the drink caused Bass to bring out Hooch, another lemon-based drink, and many other variations on this theme were bought out by all of the big manufacturing companies. Most of these brands have failed!

However, the appeal of the prepackaged 'one-shot' ready-mixed drink became obvious to spirit manufacturers among others and there has been an enormous boom in the products available. These drinks, as explained by John Foggin of Allied Domecq, are aimed at introducing the 18–25 year age group who primarily drink premium lagers (and primarily another bottled product) to the spirit market so that brand franchising can be expanded. As yet there is no evidence that these new consumers have moved to the main spirit, i.e., from Smirnoff Mule to straight Smirnoff vodka, but it is early days yet.

Ready-to-drinks tend to be lower in alcohol than the equivalent straightforward mixed drink, i.e., vodka and lemonade, and sweeter. The design of the bottle, packaging and image are very important to their main targeted segment, which is primarily young and fickle in its tastes. These beverages, such as Metz, Rigo and Red Square need to be stocked by those establishments which are aimed at the young market, for instance, pub chains such as It's A Scream, style bars like the Pitcher and Piano chain, and nightclubs. However, it should be noted that this is a very young market in terms of the product, and it is hard to say what are the classic, 'must stock' bar items since the market has only been in existence for 5 years. Therefore, given that new examples of RTDs are constantly being bought on to the market, prospective licensed house managers, while stocking some examples if they have a young consumer base, should ensure that they do not get tied into a long contract for one particular product or supplier, as one RTD may go out of favour very quickly. An eye-catching display of such products in modern glass-fronted refrigerators will help to promote sales of these beverages. (See Chapter 4 for further details.)

Deciding upon wines

In wine bars, café bars and pubs with an AB customer base, there may well be a need for the establishment to have a large wine list, rather than the more basic white dry, white medium and red selection that is suitable for many other establishments. Where this is the case there are a few points that should always be considered when setting up a new wine list, or revamping the old one. Wine lists (even if written on a chalkboard) like menus become tired if they are not updated from time to time.

1 Examine the old list, if there is one, and check what is and is not selling

2 Remember that customers will recognize certain grape varieties and regions, and these will sell fastest (unless you have the expert sales staff usually only found in specialist off-licences or up-market restaurants). This is particularly true if the wine has been the subject of a recent high visibility marketing campaign.

3 Try to choose wines attractive to your customers, rather than those you or your staff like.

4 Do not choose wines that are too young; these are an acquired taste and significant costs are involved in waiting for them to age.

5 Remember that the more attractive the nose of the wine the more it will appeal to the customer; the palate should reflect the nose.

6 Cover the taste spectrum.

7 Whites should range from a light aperitif style through to aromatic and lightly oaked to rich and full.

8 Reds should range from the light, fresh unoaked through to big and fruity, and perhaps to powerful, high tannin, very traditional food wines (if a lot of main meals are served).

9 It is often useful to include at least one sparkling wine, for those surprise celebrations that occur from time to time.

10 Arrange a tasting of the selected wines, but not too many, as most people's palates can only cope with eight to ten wines at one time.

11 Taste the wines in the venue in which they will be sold, and include as many staff, as possible in this, as they will be the ones talking to the customers.

12 Remember that the wine list does not have to cover the entire world, just a reasonable taste range; a few well-selected wines are preferable to dozens of badly selected ones.

Where there is little demand for wine, a basic dry white, medium white and one red is likely to be a sufficient range. These would normally be sourced along with other products from the wholesaler, or cash and carry. In these types of establishments it is always wise to buy well-known brands with which the customer will feel safe and the quality level is a known constant, wines such as Le Piat, Jacob's Creek, Ernest and Julio Gallo.

In either case, whether wine is a significant income generator or a minor one, the licensed house manager will have to make a decision about what size glasses they are going to use, since much of the wine will be sold by the glass. The base measures are 125 ml or 175 ml, meaning that there are six or four glasses per 75 cl bottle. However, many establishments sell wine in a double glass, i.e., either 250 ml or 350 ml (250 ml being by far the most common). The size of glass chosen must reflect the type of customers who use the establishment, and the licensed house manager needs to consider the implications of their strategy with regard to pricing and drink-driving. This is particularly relevant in light of the fact that when the unit recommendations were first set by the government, average wine strength was 9 per cent alcohol by volume (ABV), but now most new world wines easily reach 12 per cent ABV or more.

Deciding upon non-alcoholic beverages

It is a legal requirement that wherever alcoholic beverages are sold, non-alcoholic beverages must also be available, including tap water. However, it should be noted that there is a direct relationship between the sale of non-alcoholic beverages and the weather. The hotter it is, the more is sold. As Aufenast (1999) notes '"This is a very weather volatile industry" said executive chairman Robin Barr [of A. G. Barr]. . . . Forget recent trends; forget world stock markets vibrations; soft drinks producers will all just be hoping that the most health giving of properties, sunlight, shines through.'

Non-alcoholic beverages fall into seven basic categories; each is described below:

1 Carbonated or aerated water.

2 Natural spring waters, or mineral waters.

3 Squashes.

4 Juices.

5 Fresh fruit juices.

6 Syrups.

7 Non-alcoholic and low-alcohol wines and lagers.

Carbonated or aerated water • • •

These are beverages that have been 'charged' or 'aerated' with carbonic gas. That is to say that a still drink has had carbon dioxide (CO_2) added to make it fizzy. Most aerated waters are manufactured, although a few naturally still spring waters are also carbonated, e.g., Highland Spring.

Standard examples of this type of beverage always found in bars would be:

- soda water – colourless and tasteless
- tonic water – colourless and quinine flavoured
- cola – dark maroon colour, sweet herbal flavour
- ginger ale – golden straw colour, ginger flavour
- bitter lemon – pale cloudy blue colour with a very sharp lemon flavour.

There is also a wide range of carbonated or aerated waters based on fruit flavours such as orangeade, sprite, lemonade, appletiser or J2O. These move in and out of popularity and decisions about which to stock will be based on the establishment and its type of clientele.

These drinks are normally bought in bottles, either splits or babies, and come 36 or 48 to the crate, or they are bought in as syrups, pre- or post-diluted/charged and dispensed through a pump, in the same way as beer. Glass bottles are more expensive and tend to be preferred at the upper end of the market where soft drinks are usually served with an alcoholic beverage, i.e., gin and tonic. Here the customer is served the spirit and then given the bottle of soft beverage so that they can dilute the spirit to their taste. The syrup pump system tends to be used in high-volume establishments, and where there is a significant demand for non-alcoholic beverages, i.e., family venues. The larger sizes of bottles are popular in establishments such as nightclubs, for much the same reason as RTDs and bottled beers, namely that the thumb can be kept over the opening to prevent spiking. Most establishments use a combination of bulk and bottled items, the bulk for the most popular items and bottles for the less common or specialized beverages, e.g., Red Bull, a caffeine-based energy drink, or Warp.

Natural spring waters • • •

Natural spring waters come from springs in the ground. The waters are impregnated with minerals found in the rocks through which they flow. Sometimes the water may become naturally charged with an aerating gas, other waters may be still. Some still waters are artificially charged with carbonic gas. Spring waters are very popular in some parts of the world, and gaining popularity everywhere as a healthy option drink. Water of this type has been divided into two types by the EU: spring water and mineral water. Mineral water has a high mineral content and is closely regulated; spring water does not and, apart from hygiene, is affected by few regulations. Originally many of the mineral waters were drunk, or bathed in, for their medicinal properties. Table waters are a type of mineral water that tends to have a lower mineral content, and an alkaline taste. Most mineral waters were classified according to their medicinal values, however, under new stricter government regulations, all bottled mineral and spring waters now have to show their mineral content on the label.

It is suggested (*Drinks Forecast*, 2000, vol 19, no. 3) 'that per capita consumption has risen from 9.2 litres in 1994 to 11.5 litres [in 1999] and puts the total market at 624m litres with a retail value of £500m'. Table 5.1 shows the current most popular brands of non-flavoured spring waters, excluding own brands.

Waters are usually drunk on their own but can also be used to add sparkle to other drinks, for instance, some consumers prefer to add sparkling water to their spritzers instead of the more common soda water. This is an expanding market, and appeals particularly to the more sophisticated market as an alternative to fruit juice, and a suitable non-alcoholic beverage with food. Waters should always be served chilled because ice should *not* be added to the water, unless especially requested, since if a customer is trying to avoid tap water they will not want it in the form of ice. Water is usually either sold in small, 50 cl, bottles or 1-litre bottles; it is not at all common for spring water to be sold in bulk. There are two main reasons for this: first, especially with still water, it is possible for the unscrupulous person to serve tap water and charge for bottled; second, because this is the one beverage that people like to buy and share the bottle with others, especially if eating.

Some very up-market establishments make ice from spring water. In this case it could be added to the glass without asking.

Brand name	Type	Country of origin	Spring/mineral
Evian	Still	France	Spring
Highland Spring Water	Still or carbonated	Scotland	Spring
Buxton	Still or carbonated	England	Spring
Volvic	Still	France	Spring
Perrier Standard	Sparkling	France	Mineral
Vittel	Still	France	Mineral

Source: *Drinks Forecast*, 1999, vol. 19, no. 2.

Table 5.1 Bottled spring waters

Squashes, and non-alcoholic cordials • • •

These are sweetened, concentrated liquids, flavoured to taste like herbs or fruit. The cheaper versions do not necessarily contain any of the natural product the flavour resembles, i.e., orange squash may not have any orange in it. As an ever increasing amount of all baby food now sold is organic, if the establishment's main market is the family one, it may be worth using a higher-quality product that is perceived as being 'healthier and natural', although consumer perception of what is healthier and natural may depend upon public image rather than the contents of the package. For instance, Sunny Delight, a squash that looks like a fruit drink, was launched in April 1999 with a £5 million advertising campaign, and is now approximately the third best-selling brand in the UK, along with Robinsons and Ribena (*Drink Forecast*, 1999, vol 19, no. 3). It contains just 5 per cent fruit juice.

Where the main use of the squash is as a flavoured addition to alcohol the source of the flavouring may be irrelevant to the consumer. These beverages are intended to be used as flavouring in mixed drinks, or drunk diluted with water or soda water. Common bar examples are:

- orange squash

- lemon squash

- lime juice cordial

- peppermint cordial

- blackcurrant cordial.

This type of beverage is not normally a major purchase item, and may move very slowly, therefore it is usually purchased in 75 cl bottles, and a 'nominal' charge added to the purchase price of the final beverage.

Juices • • •

These are flavoured drinks containing more or less fruit/vegetable from the appropriate plant. Generally the higher the percentage of pure fruit/vegetable juice, the higher the price. The licensed house manager also has to consider the different shelf lives of the different mixes, i.e., how fast the product turns over is likely to have a significant effect upon which brand of product in which type of container to buy.

The most common juices, which are essential to all bars, are orange, grapefruit, pineapple and tomato. However, other juices are gaining in popularity, and, especially in family venues, e.g., apple-based drinks are often seen as a healthier alternative to orange juice. Cranberry and mixed juices, i.e., orange and mango, are also popular.

These juices come in 'babies', splits, cans or cartons generally. They are not normally dispensed via a pump, being very thick, and liable to clog the system. As with aerated and carbonated beverages, at the quality personalized service end of the market babies are most useful, splits or 50 cl bottles are useful where the consumer wants to drink directly from the bottle, and cartons are used for bulk demand. Cans are useful for consumption outside the premises, i.e. beer gardens or other outdoor events.

Fresh fruit juice

These are fruit juices that are squeezed upon the premises, usually to order. They have nothing else added to them, except perhaps sugar to the customer's order.

The most common fresh fruit juices are orange, lemon and grapefruit, because these citrus fruits do not require significant specialist equipment to produce them.

A niche market is developing in which establishments may serve other fresh drinks, often known as smoothies, such as apple, melon and carrot. However, specialized equipment is needed to extract the juice, and as these juices are produced from normal food sources there may be implications with regard to food safety regulations. These juices are usually served in establishments where health is a primary concern, and it may be that the establishment does not serve alcoholic beverages.

The product is bought in whole as with any other fresh food product, and squeezed either in bulk, or upon demand. Any waste juice obviously has to be thrown away at the end of service and so, while there is significant demand for this product in some venues, this is not a major product in most licensed trade premises. Staff should never confuse the term 'fruit juice' with 'fresh fruit juice'.

Syrups

These are very, very sweet concentrated fruit, nut and herb flavourings used in the making of cocktails, fruit cups and, in some cases, as the base flavouring for milk shakes. They are

Syrup	Origin
Grenadine	Pomegranate
Cassis	Blackcurrant
Citronelle	Lemon
Gomme	White sugar syrup
Framboise	Raspberry
Cerise	Cherry
Orgeat	Almond
Menthe	Mint

Table 5.2
Syrups commonly used in beverage provision

rarely drunk on their own because they are so sweet. Some syrups have an alcoholic version, e.g., grenadine and cassis. These beverages are generally only found in cocktail bars or where cocktails form a significant part of the product.

In some counties it is common for children to drink a non-alcoholic syrup diluted with still or sparkling water or soda water rather than a squash or cordial.

Non-alcoholic and low-alcohol wines and beers ● ● ●

Definition:

- Non-alcoholic – 0 per cent ABV

- Alcohol free – less than 0.05 per cent ABV

- Dealcoholized – less than 0.5 per cent ABV

- Low alcohol – 0.5–1.2 per cent ABV

- Reduced alcohol – 1.2–5.5 per cent ABV.

Alcohol is removed by distillation, arrested fermentation, dilution or reverse osmosis. Distillation is heating to remove the alcohol by evaporation. Arrested fermentation is stopping fermentation as soon as it reaches the required alcohol level, but this leaves rather a sweet drink. Dilution is the addition of water to reduce the alcoholic strength, and reverse osmosis is a process whereby the fermented liquid is passed across a special membrane that separates the alcohol from the rest of the liquid. A beverage may only be described as reduced alcohol if the original beverage was fermented to above 8 per cent ABV.

The provision of any of the alcohol-free, low-alcohol drinks would be the same as for their alcoholic equivalent.

It is very, very important for all bar staff to know which drinks contain alcohol and which do not. Alcohol-free drinks contain alcohol, all be it in minute quantities. However if, for instance, a customer has an allergy, or is taking medication, or has religious beliefs which ban the consumption of alcohol or is a under age, then it is both illegal and unethical to serve such people any product which contains even the slightest amount of alcohol.

Sources of supply

As previously noted, wherever alcoholic beverages are sold, non-alcoholic beverages must also be sold. Therefore, many of the suppliers of alcoholic beverages will also sell non-alcoholic beverages and, for convenience, non-alcoholic beverages will normally be stored in the same area and under the same conditions as the main alcoholic beverages.

Where a venue is part of a chain, be it national or regional, it is likely to be contracted into using only those suppliers nominated by the head office purchasing department. If the venue is also tied into a brewery company such as Bass, Whitbread or Brains, then the beer will come from the parent company and other beverages from nominated suppliers. These companies will have been chosen by the purchasing department because, in return for buying all of a certain product from that supplier (i.e., bulk purchasing), the supplying company will give significant discounts to the purchasing company. When businesses are independent they are free to choose any supplier they like, and negotiate what discounts they can. The irony here is that an independent chain on an expansion programme, such as J. D. Wetherspoons, which is not tied to any brewery, may be able to negotiate a better discount for products like beer from the regional brewery than that brewery's own tied tenants receive.

A description of the main methods used to purchase alcoholic beverages follows. Which method, or combination, is used depends upon the business profile; is it a destination venue, primarily selling RTDs and premium beers? Is it a family business selling a lot of draught beers and lager plus non-alcoholic beverages? Is it tied, managed or a free house?

Breweries

Breweries can be national or regional or a local microbrewery (beer brewed on site primarily for patrons' consumption). Tied houses, as previously discussed, will be tied into buying from their parent company, although they may be free to source their guest beer independently. Non-tied premises can buy from any source, and will negotiate the best discount that they can. National or regional breweries usually offer a range of beers, and the large national chains are also likely to be able to brew several foreign beers under licence. Microbreweries are likely to be much more limited in their range, and concentrate on cask ales for consumption in the locality. Some microbreweries have been designed so that they are part of the pub, as in the Mash and Air chain, and brew primarily just for that outlet.

Cash and carry

This type of operation is like a very specialist supermarket, where items can only be bought in bulk. There are no frills, the range being limited to what is available on the day, and items are paid for in cash as the buyer leaves. This type of supplier is used most regularly by small independent venues such as small local pubs that mainly sell beer and use a brewery for their beers and, perhaps, mixers. They use the cash and carry when they need to stock up on spirits and wine, because they can buy one or two bottles as and when they need to. They are also likely to use the cash and carry for dry goods, such as toilet paper, and snack items, such as crisps.

General wholesalers

These are large companies that buy from overseas and have large warehouses full of beverages, such as Grants of St James. They will stock a whole range of drinks and, in many cases, make the white spirits, such as house gin and vodka. They will often hold the distribution rights for mixers, such as Coca-Cola, Schweppes and Canada Dry. They will probably also carry some basic wines. Many on-trade premises may use wholesalers to source their spirits, premium beers, RTDs, mixers, etc. They would then use specialists for their draught beers and wines (if applicable). A tied house, while sourcing much of its output, especially beer, from the parent company, would use a wholesaler for other items.

Wine wholesaler

A wine wholesaler is like a general wholesaler, but specializes in better quality wines and, in some cases, premium spirits, such as Avery's of Bristol. This type of supplier is likely to be used by those independent venues whose customers have a higher socioeconomic profile and, therefore, disposable income. Chains with significant wine sales will also use wine wholesalers, such as Matthew Clarke.

Wine brokers

These are people who specialize in the sale of wines, normally from a specific region, and sell either to small wine wholesalers, or directly to companies which have a high demand for wine, such as the Pitcher and Piano chain. Wine brokers have good contacts in a specific region and are able to find and source large quantities, high-quality and/or rare wines. There are very few independent on-trade establishments that would deal directly with wine brokers as well as other suppliers because it is very time-consuming, unless they happened to have good quality wine lists and be known for the quality and diversity of their wines. A few wine bars may fall into this category, but it is unusual.

One reason that establishments that do not specialize in the sales of wines avoid using brokers is because of the quite complex costs involved, such as currency movements, and technical details such as the licences needed to import into the EU. For a small business the time needed to sort this out may wipe out any cost savings.

The example in Table 5.3 illustrates the point.

Vin de Pays	Wine wholesaler	Venue direct
Order size in cases	1540	140
FFr per case	84	105
@ spot rate of £1 = FFr9	£9.33	£11.76
Shipping per case	£0.80	£2.00
Duty	£12.64	£12.64
Warehouse handling	£0.60	
Delivery	£1.50	
Subtotal	£24.87	£26.31
(Finance cost 9% over 15 weeks)		£0.66
Margin over cost	20%	
Total cost to venue	£29.85	£26.97

Source: The knowledge section, *Harpers*, 16 May 1997.

Table 5.3
Costs of shipping wine direct versus buying from a wholesaler

If the purchaser buys from the wholesaler or distributor because they bring wine and bottled beer over in bulk, these costs are reduced and a small operator's time is saved. The purchaser also has someone to whom they can return any faulty items and easily claim a refund. This is an important consideration, especially to the small independent operator.

Agency distributor or brand owner

This would be the reverse of the wine broker. Here the producers have retained control over their products, and have their own marketing department to sell them. These products are usually at the premium end of the market. It is quite common for the producer to brand their products for specific markets, i.e., one brand will go to a supermarket, another to the restaurant trade, another to the on-trade. This way the producer is able to ensure that a specific brand is sold only in the type of outlet they consider suitable for it, and they are able to maintain their market share. Premium bottled beers and wine are the products most commonly sourced via this method.

Agents, distributors and large wholesalers often have licences to make many of the international brands other than wine, cask ale and deluxe spirits within the UK. As a result it is often cheaper and simpler to buy from them, rather than from 'source'. This, coupled with a suitable after sales service, often makes them a much more attractive supplier than sourcing independently.

Selecting the supplier/s

It can be seen that each establishment normally uses more than one source for their beverage supplies, e.g., a brewery plus a wholesaler or a wholesaler plus distributors. Where possible most businesses follow the usual good practice of having more than one supplier for each type of product, a major and a minor one so that if anything goes wrong with the major supplier they can still source from the minor supplier. If this is not possible, perhaps because of discount availability or speciality of product, it is wise to check that the one supplier, for instance, the brewery, could supply some mixers if another supplier, perhaps the wholesaler, was unable to deliver that day for some reason. This obviously does not apply in the case of tied houses that can only use the one source for beers. Licensed house managers, in this case, need to be very efficient in their ordering.

Before signing a contract, or making the decision to use a cash and carry, the licensed house manager should follow normal purchasing practises. An outline system could be as shown in Table 5.4.

Maintenance of beverages

It must be remembered that although some beverages such as spirits, liqueurs and some 'classical' wines have remarkably long shelf lives, and some like Madeira are almost indestructible, in legal terms beverages are classified alongside food and come under the same health and safety regulations. Control of Substances Hazardous to Health Regulations (COSHH) and the various food safety Acts are just as applicable to beverages as to food. In particular, these regulations can be very important in terms of the cellar and other storage areas, and COSHH applies with particular relevance to the service of pump beers and the cleaning and maintenance of the beer lines. It should not be forgotten that ice is also considered to be a food substance. The rationale behind this thinking, of course, is that beverages, like food, will be consumed by the customer and must be maintained and served so that they are fit for human consumption.

All cellar/storage areas should be clean and dry. Damp conditions can cause deterioration of labels and cartons, which will affect the presentation of the beverage to the customer. The lighting, whilst being safe, should be low (40 watts maximum), since extreme or rapid changes in light levels can 'shock' products which have some bottle development, such as beers and wines. A beer cellar temperature should be between 13°C and 14°C; a wine storage cellar should be at 13°C. A slight variation on either side will not affect the beverages, but significant variations of more that 3°C or 4°C either way can cause deterioration. The temperature is much more critical for beers

Stages	Activity	Details	Points to note
1	Decide what beverages are most likely to sell in that particular establishment		This depends on current sales and current and future customer requirements
2	Create purchasing specifications	This is a detailed description of the item it is intended to buy, i.e., Original Strength Plymouth Gin in 70 cl bottle at 41.2% ABV	The specification must include maximum and minimum buying amounts for each item, delivery dates and times, and price.
3	Send out the specifications to a number of suitable potential suppliers	One specification can, for beverages, cover several different beverages of a similar type, i.e., the house gin, vodka and whisky	Some of those asked to quote will not respond either because they are unable to meet the specification or through inefficient business practice
4	Choose a suitable mix of suppliers	Ensure that the suppliers are complementary, i.e., if one has problems with a core item another would be able to supply that product	Ensure that signing a contract with one supplier would not prevent purchasing from another minor supplier if necessary.
5	Confirm financial details	These should include discounts, credit terms, collection and accreditation of returnable empties, etc.	Prices for beverages usually remain fairly stable, unlike those for food and other perishables, so discounts are likely to be based on amount purchased and early payment dates
6	Confirm the collection procedure for empties	Beer kegs and casks, and the bottles and crates used for babies, are all returnable and the establishment is credited when these items are returned to the supplier	One significant area for loss of income is not returning, and/or not being credited correctly by the supplier for those items returned
7	Confirm the length of the contract	It is also often useful to know how the contract can be cancelled if needs be	A contract is usually signed for between 1 to 2 years. If it is too long the supplier may put less effort into servicing the contract. If it is too short, too much time is taken up by the management negotiating new contracts
8	Confirm everything in writing	Particularly important, for example, if only specific vintages of wine, or specific brands for house wine are required	Confusion usually arises when one party is not supplying the other party with precisely what they want when they need it. The resulting unreliable supply system can cause havoc to the business

Table 5.4 Outline system for sourcing supplies

and wines than for other products, because of alcohol levels, sugar levels or pasteurization, or all three. Therefore most establishments will ensure that the cellar temperature suits the beer and wine, and then store the other products in the same area. The area must always be kept clean and tidy, swept and washed out regularly. Empties must not be kept in the same place as the new stock because bacteria start to accumulate in the open bottles and used kegs/casks, and this can transfer itself on to and into unopened products. The storage space must be large enough to store items safety and hygienically, but not so large that it encroaches into space which could be more profitably used as a customer area.

Because the financial investment in the wet stock is huge, security of stock is of the utmost importance. A great deal of planning must be done with regard to issues such as: who has access to the cellars; the written records of all movements of stock, damage, or off-stock details; the maximum and minimum stock levels required; the physical access to the cellars, both internally and externally; the storage of the returnable bottles and kegs/casks. All these points need to be given very careful consideration if the landlord is to minimize wastage and loss, run an efficient service to his/her customers and not keep capital tied up unnecessarily.

Stock rotation must be practised, and care must be taken with those products that have 'best before' dates, to ensure that when goods are received the 'best before' dates are checked, as goods cannot be sold on to the customer if they are out of date. Not all beverages have 'best before' dates, but most beers, RTDs and non-alcoholic beverages do; all beverages have an optimum life span.

The service areas themselves must be kept clean and tidy, and all glassware and other items used to prepare and serve drinks must be pristine. A dirty or sticky glass does untold damage to the image of the establishment. Image is also seriously damaged when bar staff observe other bad practices such as handling the glasses by the top third, which 'belongs' to the customer as they must drink from it.

Further reading re the technical details of maintenance of beverages is suggested at the end of the chapter.

Pricing of beverages

Whatever system is used to price any type of beverage or food the most important point for licensed house managers to determine is the aimed for gross profit margin on sales, and how much actual money they need/want to make over a given period. The police and magistrates often look unfavourably upon some systems commonly used to boost income in quiet periods, such as 'happy hours'. This is because, if not managed well, they can cause excessive amounts of alcohol to be consumed during the period, thereby causing drunkenness. Therefore, any promotional activity considered should bear in mind that if the promotion is thought to increase antisocial behaviour it may affect the renewal of the liquor licence.

Although this section gives examples of how to price different items, it should be borne in mind that the end price to the consumer will be affected by the individual overheads of each establishment. For instance, a lease or purchase is likely to be more expensive per square metre in a busy city centre than in a suburban area. What competitors are charging will also affect the price that can realistically be obtained. This is where the professional expertise/judgement of the licensed house manager comes into play.

Beers

Beers, lagers and cider are generally purchased either by the barrel or by the bottle, and the price of a pint to the consumer can range from £1.40 in a working men's club to £3.50 in a destination venue nightclub. Cans are not considered particularly suitable for on-trade premises because consumers make direct price analysis with supermarket prices and forget on-trade overheads. Where there is a significant 'carry out' trade, cans may be sourced.

Barrel • • •

It is necessary to know:

- the size of the barrel
- the real cost of the barrel (take into account discount, etc.)
- amount credited on the return of empty barrels
- gross profit required
- current VAT rate.

A simple calculation could be as shown in Table 5.5. It should be noted that whilst draught beers are still sold in imperial measures, bottled beers are sold in metric measures.

Barrel size	barrel: 36 gallons = 288 pints
Cost of barrel	£230.40
Cost per pint	£ 0.80
Plus gross profit required	£ 0.99
	£ 1.79
Plus VAT	£ 0.31
Customer price	£ 2.10

Table 5.5
Pricing draught beer, lager and cider from the barrel

In this example the gross profit on the barrel is £285.12, however, if the barrels were not returned or stolen, then at the end of the year the brewery is likely to charge £35 for each missing barrel. If an establishment uses an average of 400 barrels per year and fails to return 5 per cent of the barrels, this would result in a loss of £700. The profit will also be reduced by any wastage, when the pipes are cleaned or excessive fobbing at the dispenser, for example. The normal loss during pipe-cleaning should be kept to the minimum, and must be covered in the gross profit required calculation.

Bottle · · ·

A similar calculation can be made for bottled beers, lagers or ciders, providing that the following are known:

- the number of bottles in the crate or carton
- the real cost of the package (taking into account discounts, etc.)
- amount credited on the return of the crate and empties (where applicable)
- gross profit required
- current VAT rate.

Standard half-pint bottles, basic IPAs and light ales, for instance, come 24 to the crate, but premium beers, where the bottle sizes differ considerably, can vary between six, nine, twelve and 24 to the package.

Spirits and liqueurs

The standard size of a spirit bottle is 70 cl. A fairly common larger bottle size, found in house spirits perhaps, is the 1 litre bottle, with 35 cl. for the half bottle. Specialized spirits or liqueurs may come in slightly different sized bottles, and the calculation of profit would need to take this into account. Most spirits are required by law to be sold in multiples of 25 ml or 35 ml. While liqueurs and liqueur/fortified wines (e.g., port) do not have a specific measure, most establishments use the standard spirit measure for these beverages so that precise profit can be calculated, to reduce wastage, and to ensure that each customer gets the same blend each time (in a beverage such as Malibu and coke for instance). An example of costing a house spirit (in this case, gin) is given in Table 5.6, costing other spirits, liqueurs or liqueur/fortified wines uses the same principle.

In England and Wales most establishments use 25 cl as the base measure, in Scotland and the Channel Islands 35 cl is generally used as the base measure. If 35 cl were the base measure then the

Size of bottle	70 cl
House base spirit measure	25 cl
Measures per bottle	28
Cost per bottle	£7.50
Cost per measure	£0.27
Plus gross profit required	£0.72
	£0.99
Plus VAT	£0.21
Customer price	£1.20

Table 5.6
Pricing spirits

calculation would be based upon 20 measures to the bottle. Some bars are doubles bars; in this case the base measure used is 50 cl or 70 cl. As these are not common the fact that the establishment is a doubles bar must be clearly stated so that the customer can make decisions about the price–quality relationship, as well as considering their overall consumption of alcohol. Generally aromatized wines, such as Martini or Dubonnet, and liqueur/ fortified wines, such as port or sherry, are sold in double measures, i.e., in multiples of 50 cl, therefore there are only 14 standard measures in a bottle.

Alcoholic carbonates and RTDs

Alcoholic carbonates and RTDs are purchased by the bottle, therefore, the pricing considerations are the same as for bottled beers.

Wines

There are two main methods of pricing the bottles on a wine list: gross profit percentage and cash gross profit.

Gross profit percentage · · ·

Traditionally gross profit percentage was used, and indeed still is, in some establishments which have not moved with the times, or which only sell 'house' wines. Gross profit percentage means adding the same amount of gross profit to each wine, see Table 5.7.

Cost price	Gross profit %	Gross profit (£)	Selling price (£)	+ VAT = (£)	Wine list price (£)
4.00	60	6.00	10.00	1.75	11.75
8.00	60	12.00	20.00	3.50	23.50
14.00	60	21.00	35.00	6.13	41.13

Table 5.7
Wine pricing using gross profit percentage

This was the usual pricing method before customers became better educated and more aware about wine, during the 1990s. Nowadays consumers are much more aware about what wine costs in the supermarket, off-licence or from their wine merchant, and while they also know that overheads in the on-trade are higher that in retail outlets they are able to make a value judgement about what constitutes a reasonable profit.

As previously mentioned, some wine producers produce two or more versions of a similar wine, one for the off-trade, and one for the on-trade, etc. This is to stop customers making direct comparisons. But just as the prospective licensed house manager is able to make judgements about the price–quality relationship of wine, so are their increasingly sophisticated customers.

Cash gross profit

This is where the same amount of cash profit is added on to each bottle of wine, see Table 5.8.

Most establishments are moving away from gross profit percentage to cash gross profit, since they have found that if customers perceive the wine to be good value, they will either trade up or buy an extra bottle, or possibly even do both. However, if the customers think that they are being overcharged they will go for the lowest cost wine, and spend the least possible amount, even, while eating, quenching their thirst with tap water.

It is true to say that many efficiently run establishments use a mixture of both systems. House wines and those just one step above are usually on a gross profit percentage; above that cash gross profit is used, although if very expensive wines are sold, (say at £100 per bottle upwards) the establishment will probably have a tiered system of cash gross profit, see Table 5.9. (It is rare to find on-trade premises selling wine at this price level, but it is not unknown especially in some exclusive private members clubs.)

From Table 5.9 it can be seen that the highest profit level percentage is made on the house wine. This is because the majority of sales will be house wines, and therefore it is sensible to make the most profit on the product with the fastest turnover.

Cost price (£)	Gross profit (£)	Selling price (£)	+ VAT = (£)	Wine list price (£)
4.00	6.00	10.00	1.75	11.75
8.00	6.00	14.00	2.45	16.45
14.00	6.00	20.00	3.50	23.50

Table 5.8
Wine pricing using cash gross profit

Table 5.9
Wine pricing using a mixed
pricing structure

	House wine	Mid-range wine	Premium wine
Cost	£ 3.00	£8.00	£ 80.00
Gross profit required	70%	£10.00	£ 25.00
Selling price	£10.00	£18.00	£105.00
+ VAT	£ 1.75	£ 3.15	£ 23.40
Wine list price	£11.75	£21.15	£128.40

Pricing wine by the glass • • •

The legal measures for wine by the glass are either 125 ml or 175 ml. Depending upon which measure the establishment chooses, since a standard wine bottle is 75 cl, there are either six or four (+) glasses per bottle. The pricing calculation method is then as for spirits.

Some establishments sell wine as a 'glass', 'large glass' or 'double'. Sometimes the smaller and larger measures are the standard legal measures, 125 ml and 175 ml; however in some establishments the standard glass may be 175 ml and the larger measure 350 ml (2 × 175 ml). This management decision has obvious implications for pricing the wine, but there are also social issues, such as drink-driving, to be considered since one 350 ml 'glass' is in fact nearly half a bottle of wine (see Chapter 8).

Selling wine by the glass is the norm in on-trade establishments other than restaurants, but in traditional establishments the range can be very limited. In some of these traditional establishments it may be worth considering expanding the range of wines by the glass since the gross profit percentage is very high and is consumption rising. Many establishments which do not have large wine sales, now buy wine in the same way as spirits, one house white and one premium brand white, for instance, and price accordingly.

Non-alcoholic beverages

Non-alcoholic beverages, apart from squashes and syrups, are generally bought by the bottle or dispensed on draught as discussed previously in this chapter. Therefore, they are generally priced with the same considerations as for beer, including returns where applicable. The amount credited on the return of non-alcoholic beverages can be very significant. The average price of a crate of 48 baby mixers, orange juice for instance, is £5.80. The amount credited for a full crate of empties returned is £3.50, meaning that the contents of the bottles cost £2.30 or 5p per bottle as opposed to 12p per bottle before the returns. If the establishment sells 400 crates per year, not returning where applicable could result in an unnecessary loss of around £1400 per annum.

Squashes and syrups are usually used as small additives to another beverage, which will be charged at full price, e.g., lager and lime. The amount charged for these beverages, therefore, is notional. A bottle of squash may cost up to 50p; each shot in the glass may be charged at anything between 10p and 20p, depending upon management philosophy, and anywhere between fifteen and thirty measures may be extracted from each bottle depending, for example, upon whether they are used as the base for a squash drink on a hot day, or solely as shots in a lager. If sales of pints of squash become significant then the pricing structure of pints of squash would have to be reviewed since if the customer is drinking a low-priced pint of squash they are not drinking a normally priced pint of beer and the gross profit margin will have decreased significantly.

Section 1 summary propositions

1 Whilst beer is generally the most significant beverage sold, getting the combination of other beverages right confirms the image and consumer perception of an establishment.

2 The return of empties and control of ullage is critical in maintaining the required profit margins.

3 The suppliers chosen must be suitable for the type of establishment.

Section 1 summary questions

1 What type of establishment, with what type of customers would serve mainly: (a) draught beers; (b) bottled premium beers and (c) RTDs and alcoholic carbonates. Why?

2 In a local pub what would be suitable house and premium brands for each of the following spirits: gin, whisky, vodka, rum and brandy?

3 What would be a reasonable buying and selling price for these products?

4 What would be the likely rationale used when deciding what range of wines to serve in a city-centre café bar?

5 What type of establishment sells smoothies, and who would be the likely target market?

Section 2: Food provision and services

Food in bars and pubs

Historically food provision was an important part of the provision in inns, however, as pubs and restaurants separated in the eighteenth and nineteenth centuries, food became totally unimportant in pubs, until the introduction of the Beer Orders (see Chapter 3). Since then the provision of food in all types of licensed trade premises has grown phenomenally, from almost zero, to up to 40 per cent of sales. As well as the Beer Orders there are a multitude of factors which have to be considered to explain this phenomenon.

General economic factors, such as increasing personal disposable income levels, falling unemployment rates and the increase in dual income families, have resulted in increased consumer confidence. Research conducted by Mintel show that the variation in demand could also be explained by changes in the age profile, with an increase in younger consumers as well as a significant increase in the family and the grey consumer. Most importantly, as more households than ever have both adults in full-time work and more disposable income, they have less time and inclination to prepare meals (Mintel, 1999). However, there are regulatory factors that may influence the market in the near future, such as the White Paper currently being considered by the government, with regard to the potential relaxation of licensing laws, the introduction and increase of the statutory minimum wage and the effect of the implementation of the EU Working Hours Directive.

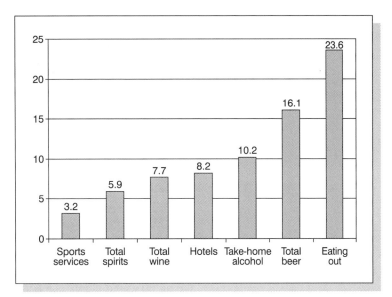

Figure 5.1
UK eating-out market (£ billion at current prices)
Source: ONS data adjusted by Whitbread to include business and foreign tourist expenditure, 1999.

The importance of catering to the industry cannot be under-estimated, currently worth £5 billion in food sales a year, £1 billion more than 5 years ago and £1 billion less than the spending predictions for 2001. More than 18 million people regularly eat out in pubs and 80 per cent of people consider pubs to be better value for money than restaurants, wine bars and fast-food chains (Mintel, 1999). Pubs serve an average of 3.5 million meals a day; 8 million eat Sunday lunches one Sunday in four, usually as a family. The second busiest day of the year is Valentine's Day, with the most popular single busiest day being Mother's Day, especially since the licensing laws were relaxed in 1995.

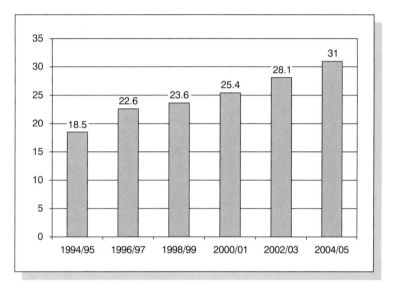

Figure 5.2
UK eating-out market forecasts 1994–5 to 2004–5 (£ billion at current prices)
Source: ONS data adjusted by Whitbread to include business and foreign tourist expenditure, 1999.

The large players have targeted specific groups of the population, using their promotional and marketing expertise to sell branded products. The big brewers have invested heavily in promoting brand loyalty, which in turn has caused the estab-lished fast-food operators to market heavily in order to maintain their market position.

In 1998, £15 billion will be spent by consumers in the UK on eating out. This figure has risen by over a quarter compared with 1993, although in real terms the increase is more modest, at around 4%. Growth has been across the board, with sales of fast food and those of more traditional restaurant food growing at a similar pace. Although fast food has a very high profile, it still accounts for less than one third of total spending on eating out, with spending on traditional meals in a restaurant and pub catering account-ing for the vast majority of the total (Mintel, 1998).

The diversity of food

The revolution both in types of licensed trade premises, and of the food provision within them, in the last decade has led to millions of ordinary people discovering that these venues cannot be beaten for value for money, convenience and informality, whether for a quick bar snack, a family meal or a high-class meal to rival any restaurant. The quality of food in some of the privately-owned establishments has reached such a high standard that the *Michelin Guide* has created a new section offering critical acclaim. Many of the country's leading chefs work within the licensed trade, as this often gives them the opportunity to work as chef patron, unaffordable to most in the conventional restaurant trade.

Branded food

The popularity of branded catering is indisputable, with new concepts and ideas being developed all the time. Some of the many benefits of a branded chain are:

- brand loyalty can be transferred nationally and internationally
- financial advantages of centralized menu planning, leading to bulk purchasing of ingredients and standardization of quantities
- marketing strategies to the mass media, customers response to products and promotional campaigns
- standardization of the operational systems
- training programmes can be prepared nationally, allowing staff to work in all outlets
- product development can be efficiently resourced
- companies such as Whitbread or Bass spend considerable sums of money on corporate branding in food and beverage.

However, branding is not without constraints, particularly regarding the opportunity for individuality and regional specialities. This is so despite the use of 'specials of the day' as an attempt to address the issue. Concept branding can be described as frozen food and identical menus, relying on multi-portion products prepared in conjunction with frozen food suppliers. Matthew Moggridge, editor of the *Pub Food Magazine* writes: 'For good pub food, steer clear of branded pub restaurant chains and urban/suburban pubs with huge laminated menu's, they are invariably brewery owned, managed houses which care more about bottled premium lagers than the standard of food on offer' (*Pub Industry Handbook*, 1999).

Quality food pubs

Thirty years ago, a ploughman's lunch, chicken and chips or a sandwich were considered culinary excellence. The quality market has improved so dramatically that there are now over 100 pubs in the *Michelin Guide*. For example, of the many distinguished chef patrons preferring to run a pub to a restaurant, not least is Chris Barber, who was personal chef to Prince Charles, and currently serves high-quality food at the Goose in Birtwell Salome, Oxfordshire. Alan Reid of the Wheatsheaf, Swinton, on the Scottish Borders, won the first Taste of Scotland and Scottish Seafood Award in 1998 with a 'Supreme of halibut with a crab, coriander and cous-cous crust and herb-scented leeks with red pepper coulis'. Dishes available in these types of outlets include many with local roots, such as 'Evesham Pie (beef with plums and plum wine)' at the Crown and Trumpet, Broadway, Worcestershire, and 'Pencarreg Blue Cheese tartlets' from the Drover's Arms, Howey in Powys. International dishes such as Californian rabbit, Thai pork tenderloin and Mexican burritos are just a small sample of the eclectic cuisine available. Michael Bateman writes 'We're seeing the rise of the gastro-pub rather than the restaurant' (*Independent on Sunday*, 22 August 1999). The symbol of the fork and a foaming tankard

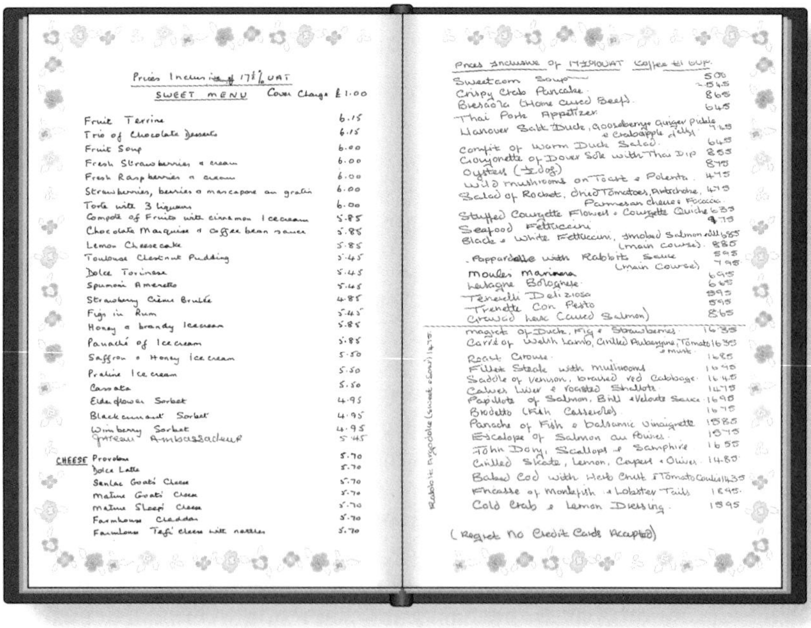

Figure 5.3 Menu from The Walnut Tree Inn, Llandewi Skirrid, Abergavenny, Gwent

used by the *Michelin Guide* looks set to become a sought after and recognized award. Susan Nowak has been producing a CAMRA guide to pubs that provide good food for 10 years, and the latest (fifth edition) lists 600 pubs.

Vegetarian food

Consumer demand for vegetarian food is increasing. Nineteen per cent of respondents to a recent Mintel report claimed to be choosing vegetarian dishes, despite not actually being vegetarians. Major influences in reducing the amount of meat consumed, such as ethical and green issues, has meant that 5 million consumers are modifying their diet in some way. A 'real eat' survey in 1997 revealed a 20 per cent increase in vegetarians since 1995, with some sources believing it to be as high as 10 per cent of the population, with 3 per cent being vegan.

It would be very unusual today for a menu to offer no meat-free dishes, with most establishments being aware that the consumer (vegetarian or not) is expecting a greater choice, to keep in touch with new retail products and food trends. Café bars and other venues at the cutting edge of fashion are likely to go much further than conventional pubs in the provision of vegetarian, vegan and other ethnic meals.

Catering for the family

Pubs and pub restaurants emerged as attracting over half of all family respondents, reflecting many pub operators' family friendly offer. Family friendly brands, such as Whitbread's Brewer's Fayre and Allied Domecq's Big Steak, are leading the family eating out market with extensive facilities for children such as stand alone play areas and children's clubs. (Mintel, 1998)

Family consumers prefer to eat where their children are welcome, and in a relaxed and informal atmosphere. Parents are strongly influenced by children – 'pester power' – which often leads to parents sacrificing the quality of food they would prefer in deference to their children's demands, and family harmony. The quality of children's menus are often subject to criticism, as they mainly consist of chips, with burgers, fish fingers, chicken nuggets and a limited vegetarian offering. The standards of children's menus will need to improve to meet the demands of the parents and children as demand grows and expectations expand.

Figure 5.4 Drover's Feast menu

Theme pub

Themed pubs are a relatively new phenomenon, with little or no historical evidence of them before 1992. It is generally acknowledged that the first genuine 'Sports bar' was opened in 1993 and with 'Irish pubs', the first multiple chains began in 1994. Theme pubs, which have been converted, are thought to have increased turnover by approximately 30 per cent. Mintel (1999) estimates the average town and city-centre pub to have a turnover of £8500 per week (it is in this type of location that themed pubs are to be found), which on average increases to £11 000 after conversion. Sports bars enjoy an even higher level of turnover by comparison, because most of them are over 3000 sq. ft, which is three to four times larger than the average pub – the average is £30 000 per week, with some larger sites turning over £100 000 a week. Due to their size, the atmosphere created makes them a fun place to be, which in turn increases drink and food turnover. Themed pubs are increasing in popularity, with many innovative ideas on the horizon. The viability of such venues will depend on investment, research, planning, design, training, service standards and meeting customer expectations.

Food safety and hygiene and kitchen design

Having established that food is an integral part of the majority of pubs, café bars, bars and wine bars, food safety and hygiene is of paramount importance. Food and beverage managers need to be familiar with the concept of hazard analysis critical control point (HACCP) which is now regarded as a very effective method of controlling food safety and hygiene. The Food Standards Agency (FSA) is also expected to force environmental health officers to tighten up on the enforcement of regulations within these venues. Local authorities enforcing health and safety regulations will be backed up financially by the FSA.

The FSA works as a watchdog to:

- issue general guidelines on how to cook safely

- advise ministers when to take action over food scares

- consult everyone on health risks

- ensure a more consistent approach to enforcement by local authorities

- impose a registration system for food outlets (*Brands Food and Catering*, 1998).

'The creation of an independent government body to work toward improving the standards and quality of food production in the UK and in all sectors is an attempt to improve food safety in the next millennium' (Kinton *et al.*, 1996: 517)

Design

'Kitchens are now fully equipped and demand the appropriate level of investment – a microwave and a deep fat fryer are no longer adequate' (Davis *et al.*, 1998: 329). Given the increase in the importance of food operations, and the ever improving standards of quality and safety required, the design of the kitchen and the food service facilities must meet the following:

- customer requirements in terms of food and beverage products and service style

- projected numbers of customers, with an indication of the variation in demand throughout the year

- menu type (fixed, cyclic, market, etc.)

- menu format, structure and content

- projected sales volume for each menu item

- method of production and service for each menu item to customer's order assembled to customer's order from preprepared components or prepare in advance batches to production schedule

- quantity of food to be produced at a time
- preparation and equipment required to produce the menu item
- storage required before and during preparation and prior to service – volume of food and storage conditions
- food service concept – the form of delivery of the food/beverage product to the customer, ambience of restaurant, etc.
- method of service delivery and the nature of the interaction between the customer and the operation
- type of crockery and utensils, harmony with décor and menu
- purchasing policy for food, beverages and other consumables (Davies *et al.*, 1998: 146).

Once these factors have been considered, an outline plan can be prepared. Staffing requirements, to meet the customer requirements will depend on the effectiveness of the equipment and design. Individual establishments will have their own unique problems, which will need to be analysed, to maximize the space available.

There is a growing application of standardization in food products, with the major players becoming increasingly reliant on convenience products, which enable large companies to maintain strict levels of consistency and reliability.

The independent freeholders, who are striving for individuality, may well be designing the products, manufacturing and selling all under the one roof. As a result the food safety and hygiene in this process varies widely.

Those potential licensees interested in the provision of food are advised to study for an appropriate National Vocational Qualification/Scottish Vocational Qualification (NVQ/SVQ) and food safety and hygiene qualifications, see Chapter 9. For further technical details on the construction, sourcing and maintenance of the food production and service areas see the 'Reference and further reading' list at the end of this chapter.

Pub estates and food

A total of 319 pub estate operators (company or brewer that owns a large number of pubs) exist, with the 10 largest controlling 25 849 pubs (about 70 per cent of the total UK operations). Whitbread, as the largest operator in the licensed trade sector, is a good example of a large corporate which pioneered the revolution in pub food in the 1970s and 1980s. Whitbread are multisector operators, with interests in pizzas and pasta, the restaurant meals sector as well as its licensed trade operations. Other large brewers are also multi-sector operators, although on a lesser scale. All the big brewers, such as Bass, Scottish and Newcastle and Greenalls are actively looking to exploit new sectors of the leisure industry as the rate of growth from their traditional revenue source, brewing, has declined.

In the main, the breweries have chosen to develop their pub-restaurant eating out format. 'Whitbread's aim is to create brands which customers enjoy and appreciate and which have the potential to become leaders in their segments of the market. Although they share many behind-the-scene services, each one is clearly differentiated in the eyes of its customers' (*Whitbread Briefing Book*, 1999).

Food pricing

Some food will be bought in ready prepared, as in cook-chilled dishes. These dishes will only need to be reheated and garnished before service, and so the costing is very simple in that the required gross profit merely needs to be added to the buying price of the dish, plus a nominal sum for the garnish. This is very similar to the pricing of bottled beverages such as premium bottled beers or RTDs.

Standard recipe for the Marquis of Bute at Builth Wells: Welsh lamb casserole (10 portions)

Ingredients	Quantity	Unit cost (£)	Ingredient cost (£)
Shoulder of Welsh lamb – diced	1.8 kg	3.25	5.85
Carrots – peeled and sliced	0.25 kg	0.80	0.20
Onions – skinned and sliced	3	0.10	0.30
Sticks of celery – sliced	5	0.09	0.45
Bay leaves	2	0.05	0.10
Dried thyme	15 ml	0.02	0.30
Salt and pepper	–	–	0.10
Stock	750 ml	–	0.10
Butter	65 g	2.90	0.19
Flour	120 g	0.65	0.08
Egg yolks	3	0.09	0.27
Single cream	400 ml	2.20	0.88
Parsley – fresh and chopped	–	–	0.10
Total cost of food			8.92
Cost per portion (÷10)			0.89
Vegetables (nominal price)			0.25
Total cost of dish			1.14
Add gross profit required (60%)			1.71
Selling price of dish (before VAT)			2.85

Table 5.10 Example of standard dish costing using fresh ingredients

Other establishments will choose to make up their dishes from fresh ingredients. In this case the manager and/or chef must make up standard recipes and methods of cooking so that the exact cost of the dish can be calculated, and the required gross profit added to find the selling price. The use of standard recipes and methods of cooking will also ensure that the dish is prepared to the same standard and quality level each time, thus ensuring that customer expectations are met each time they eat in the establishment. Table 5.10 shows an example of a standard recipe calculation

The future of catering within the licensed trade environment

The future development of food as a significant revenue generator in many licensed trade establishments is likely to show steady growth. Research by Mintel (1999) indicates a number of significant factors, which augur well for the provision of catering:

1 *'Value for money and added value offers will become even more important to restaurant and pub operators in the lower to middle sector of the market.'* Consumers are likely to exercise a certain amount of caution when spending on eating out, with the level of personal disposable income rising over the last 5 years, the uncertainty of the interest rates, the rising housing market and other similar factors.

2 *'Eateries, which specifically target young consumers, will do well.'* The proportion of 35 to 44 year olds is set to increase, this is the group most likely to have children, which is a family formation that has been targeted very successfully.

3 *'Consumers are much less formal nowadays.'* Many consumers wish to eat wearing informal clothes, they do not need to be served by waiters or waitresses and often choose to snack rather than eat a family meal.

4 *'Speed of service is becoming a more important factor.'* Pubs are able to serve food quickly and efficiently.

5 *'An increase in the number of older consumers.'* The increase in the 55 to 64 age bracket, many of whom will have paid off their mortgages, are likely to be looking for a meal in pleasant surroundings.

6 *'More women in employment.'* Working mothers will have less time for cooking and more disposable income for eating out, particularly for family occasions. Pubs have targeted family catering and will gain a large part of this sector.

7 *'Marketing promotions.'* Database information is likely to be used by pub-restaurant operators for mailing lists for general occasions, such as Mother's Day, Father's Day, Easter and Christmas events, anniversaries and children's birthdays.

Conclusion

The licensed trade industry is offering such a diverse range of styles and services, which cover the whole spectrum of the consumer's needs. Consumers are becoming very open-minded about what they wish to eat, and they are looking to find new product offerings all the time. All operators need to be ready for 'the next big thing' and watch for any new developments.

Despite the immense resources at the disposal of the major operators, it seems that many of the best concepts will continue to be developed by entrepreneurs. The challenge for the majors will be to watch the progress of new concepts very closely and time their approaches so that they can acquire a business just when it is set to take off but when the existing operators do not have enough capital to develop the business at the pace they would like (Mintel, 1998).

Section 2 summary proposition

1 The volume and value of catering within licensed houses has increased significantly over the last 10 years with changes of lifestyle and stagnation of other restaurant sectors.

2 The range of pub-based food is now enormous with a very small minority only offering crisps and pies. Michelin run their own good pub food guide as do CAMRA, with many exciting and innovative dishes and menus being offered. In between, the mass-produced themed outlets offer a reasonably priced alternative to cover the gap between fast food and traditional restaurants.

3 Food hygiene and safety are issues that are ignored by owners/managers at their own peril. The design of kitchen and food areas in general requires careful thought and planning.

4 The outlook for informal catering on licensed trade premises is positive, however, in order to succeed, changes in consumer tastes, quality and value for money must be of prime concern.

Section 2 summary questions

1 Why has catering seen such a prolific growth rate in the last 10 years?

2 What factors influence a consumer to eat in a public house rather than a traditional restaurant?

3 Why is food hygiene and safety so important?

4 What themed pubs are in your area? Do you use them? Why or why not? Is specialization into one niche market limiting your customer base and making you a slave to fashion or allowing you to cash in on others ideas?

Case study 1

The French Inn is a traditional pub on Hampstead Heath in London with a good reputation for food as well as a traditional pub atmosphere. It also has an attractive beer garden. This pub has just been sold by Whitbread as a free house.

1 What effect will this change of ownership have upon the French Inn's sources of supply?

2 Is the change of ownership likely to affect the prices charged to the consumer?

3 Is the change of ownership likely to change the range of beverages and foods available to the pub's customer?

Case study 2

In Chapter 4, 'Market research' section, the case of a Cardiff chain restaurant was outlined in terms of a television exposé of the food hygiene shortcomings found there. The problems in detail were that food removed from the freezer had been stored in the fridge beyond the specified date and yet was still considered safe to eat. The use-by-date on the products was altered. Many other unlawful food-handling instances also occurred such as serving food that had fallen on the floor.

1 How would you as the new manager coming into the unit deal with the problem of the lack of consumer confidence in your food?

2 How would you ensure staff follow the correct procedures?

3 How could you assure your clientele that your food was now safe to eat?

References and further reading

Aufenast, J. (1999). Soft focus. *Harpers Wine and Spirit Weekly*, **5910**, 27–9.

Birchfield, J. C. (1988). *Design and Layout for Foodservice Facilities*. Van Nostrand Reinhold.

Caterer and Hotelkeeper (journal).

Clissold, I. (1997). *The CAMRA Guide to Cellarmanship*. CAMRA.

Davis, B., Lockwood, A. and Stone, S. (1998). *Food and Beverage Management*. 3rd edn. Butterworth-Heinemann.

Drink Forecast (2000). February, vol. 19, no. 4.

Fattorini, J. E. (1997). *Managing Wine and Wine Sales*. Thompson Business Press.

Fuller, J. and Kirk, D. (1991). *Kitchen Planning and Management*. Butterworth-Heinemann.

Harpers Wine and Spirit Weekly (journal).

Jackson, M. (1997). *Beer Companion*. 2nd edn. Mitchell Beazley.

Johnson, H. (1997). *The World Atlas of Wine*. Mitchell Beazley.

Kinton, R., Ceserani, V. and Foskett, D. (1996), *The Theory of Catering*. Hodder and Stoughton.

Kotas, R. and Jayawardena, C. (1994). *Profitable Food and Beverage Management*. Hodder and Stoughton.

Michelin Guide (1999).

Mintel Marketing Intelligence, www.mintel.co.uk (1996, 1998, 1999).

Odgers, P. (1997). *Purchasing, Costing and Control*. Stanley Thornes.

Protz, R. (1995). *The Ale Trail*. Eric Dobby.

Pub Industry Handbook (1999).

The Publican (journal).

Robinson, J. (1999). *The Oxford Companion to Wine*. 2nd edn. Oxford University Press.

Whitbread Briefing Book (1999).

Wine and Spirit Education Trust (WSET) (ed.) (1998). *Behind the Label*. Wine and Spirit Education Trust.

Managing the human resources

Introduction

This chapter will deal with the fundamental and exacting process of managing the most important resource in any licensed house, the people who will operate it. As with any service industry the staff who interact with the customers will either enhance or detract from the products, the drink, the service, the food and the overall experience of the house. They will determine whether or not the business succeeds or fails, meets the needs of the customers or leaves them with a negative impression so that they never return or, worse still, they tell everyone else about the bad staff at the public house or club. The backroom staff (the chefs, cellar staff, administration staff) are equally as important as those who come into contact with the public; their technical skills and abilities are key to the operation, without them the operation will grind to a halt.

It is essential in managing the organization that the manager considers the staff alongside such other decisions as the products they sell (see Chapter 4) or the systems they operate (Chapter 5). To this end it may be useful to give an overall objective to the process of the management of human resources within licensed premises.

The objective is to provide the right number of people, with the right skills and behaviours, at the right time in order effectively to meet the needs of the organization.

The management of the human resources, therefore, covers the process of obtaining staff, developing staff, promoting them, retaining them and rewarding them for their labour. The model in Figure 6.1 shows the different processes involved.

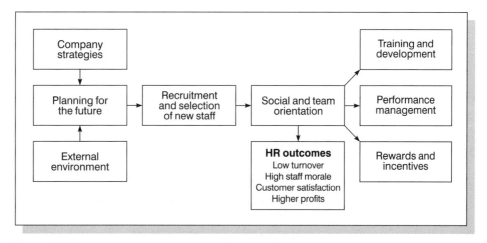

Figure 6.1 Human resource management in licensed premises

1 *The external environment*: no business exists in a vacuum, it is dependent on a number of external circumstances which affect the way in which it can or must operate. Most of these factors can be simplified into political, economic, social and technological. These PEST factors will constrain the business within laws and government actions (political), the amount of money people have to spend on the products (economic), if the products and services are morally acceptable or trendy (social) and even if the outlet is effective, responsive and profitable (technological). These factors impinge particularly on human resources through the influence they have upon the labour market that managers have to obtain their staff from. This labour market will not only determine the availability of labour but will determine how much pay staff receive, whether the unit loses staff or how much effort and money is spent on recruiting and training that staff. This market is further discussed in the next section.

2 *The company strategies*: the way in which a business deals with its human resources will also be determined by the strategies and objectives that it has for the future. In managed houses those strategies will be determined under the main companies' strategies, but even then the manager will have to operate those strategies and convert them into action. Owners will have to determine their own strategies and plans and operationalise them. Within these strategies on what products to sell, equipment to buy or marketing to carry out, the management must also determine plans for the human resources. These plans will reflect how the business will change in the short, medium and long term. If, for example, the business is going to expand, then more staff may be required. If there are to be new processes or equipment, then staff will have to be trained to use them.

3 *Recruitment and selection*: this is part of the process to control the inflow of people into the organization. It involves a series of connected processes designed, first, to advertise the vacancy and, second, to search for a suitable candidate from those who apply. It is a potential minefield for managers both from a legal and an operational perspective. The legal aspects appertain to equal opportunities and trades description legislation and a breach of these could lead to civil and criminal proceedings. The operational issues are those concerned with the time required, the organization, decision-making and the cost. We deal with these processes in more depth later in this chapter.

4 *Orientation*: once the new employee is selected you must then proceed to integrate them into the organization, train them in operational and legal aspects of the job and ensure that they settle into the set-up as quickly as possible. If you neglect this important aspect you will have staff unable to do their job and will lose staff through dissatisfaction. The processes of induction and job training are central processes here and are also dealt with later in this chapter.

5 *Training and developing staff*: training is not just a one-off process but should be a continual one. In the future you will require new supervisors, head chefs or managers, and it may be better to promote existing staff, as it will demonstrate the possibility of progression within the business. Well-trained staff will also be better staff, give better service, make better decisions and, ultimately, make you more money; untrained or badly trained staff will produce the exact opposite of these.

6 *Performance management*: throughout an employee's time with the company you will have to monitor and evaluate their work. This can be through the simple process of congratulations or correction, but to be effective it must also involve a more formal aspect. The process of appraisal allows the manager to examine with the employee their strengths and weaknesses, to identify training requirements and locate potential for advancement. It may also assist in reward systems and provide the basis for identifying problems within the business as a whole. The examination of these processes later in this chapter will also include discipline and grievance aspects of employment.

7 *Rewards and incentives*: the work–reward relationship is vitally important in the context of turnover, recruitment, development and motivation. If the pay and other benefits meet the expectations of the employee, then retention and motivation can be achieved. In other words if the wages are considered fair then the staff are able to gain satisfaction from work and take pride in it. Achieving the right balance between extrinsic (money, benefits, etc.) and intrinsic (satisfaction, recognition, social needs) reward is vital in managing any set of people.

Labour markets

The labour market for the hospitality industry as a whole epitomizes the market for the licensed trade sector. It is primarily based on flexibility, and many writers in hospitality human resource management (HRM) have demonstrated that the flexibility striven for by many other industries is present in the hospitality industry already. Where the licensed trade industry differs from the larger hospitality sector is in the size of unit and, therefore, the numbers of staff are smaller than those of most hotels and catering units. However, skills from the rest of the industry are transferable between those sectors and licensed retail. For example bar staff from hotels can easily adapt their skills to the public house trade; chefs are even more mobile.

Attributes of the labour market

Michael Riley (2000) states that hospitality labour markets contain a number of obvious features:

- a fairly large proportion of unskilled occupations

- the transferability of skills at any level between a broad range of hotel and catering establishments

- often but not invariably, high levels of labour turnover

- low levels of pay, particularly for unskilled work.

The level of unskilled jobs in the industry is not akin to those in production processes in machine minding but are 'a bundle of low level tasks which, no matter how menial require self organization' (Riley, 2000). This causes problems in trying to ally low pay levels in the industry to skill levels. If the job requires reasonably high levels of even basic skill then why is pay so depressed? The answer may seem to be within the area of excess supply of labour for these jobs. Most establishments rely on only a small core of full-time workers with peaks of demand met by managing a plethora of part-time, casual or vacational workers. The drives of these workers are those based on the accumulation of either additional income for short periods of work, work to fit in with family tasks or short-term working periods. As the industry is one of the few to allow these goals to be fulfilled this creates the surplus. One has only to think of the number of students working part time to support their studies to see this in action. The fact that in university cities the students cause the peaks may assist the house manager in management of labour supply.

Turnover

Turnover is generated by many of the particular attributes of the industry. The mobility of skills and low pay will often force workers to look for 'greener fields' elsewhere. It would thus be true that those outlets offering slightly better conditions than others around them would have lower recruitment problems and less turnover, although this will depend on the nature of the operation and the managerial style in dealing with people. The way in which managers handle their staff is another major reason for turnover in the industry. Those who treat their staff equitably with a proactive approach to their needs are likely to have lower turnover of staff compared with those who do not. Most other turnover is caused by the casual and part-time worker who either has no use for the job or who gets bored.

Retention

Retaining a positive and productive labour force is the major task facing any licensed house manager. In the absence of being able to raise basic pay, promotion, benefits and even bonuses can be used to ensure retention. However, many organizations see development as another means of not only retaining staff but also improving both quality and productivity. The main aims of the Whitbread 'badge' approach are based on this idea.

Human resource planning

The process of human resource (HR) planning, or what some textbooks still refer to as 'manpower', can be very complex or relatively straightforward, depending on a number of different factors:

1 *The overall strategy of the organization*: whether the organization is seeking to grow (plans would include recruitment, promotion, selection and training) or to shrink or downsize (redundancy, recruitment freeze, or automation) or change its products or style of service (recruitment and selection, and retraining) or retain its market and merely improve quality (development, motivation, retention). Each type of strategy will require a different human resource response, a different type of plan.

2 *The internal labour market*: whether or not the company has the people available to meet the promotions of the future, and change behaviours and ideas. Or are they incompatible with the way you want the organization to run?

3 *The external labour markets*: are there within the local or regional labour market the skills the company requires? If there are in abundance it will simplify the processes of recruitment and

selection as the company will not have to advertise vigorously to attract staff. It may also, in areas of high unemployment, mean that staff are more likely to stay as any stable job may be seen as worth keeping.

4 *The skill of the management*: whether the branch or unit manager actually knows what they are doing in terms of the planning processes or are going to 'play it by ear', deal with problems as they arrive rather than trying to foresee them and stop them from affecting the business. Part of that skill comes with experience, the rest from correct use and interpretation of the methods below.

5 *The budget allowed for the process*: the amount of money the company spends on detailed HR planning may well be restricted. This will limit not only the size of the operation but also how much detailed planning is necessary. For example, many very large companies carry out a process of cohort analysis, when a number of staff enter the organization at the same time, perhaps as trainee managers on a graduate scheme. The analysis will plot the movement of that cohort of individuals throughout their working lives with the company – promotion, development, demotion, dismissal, resignation, etc. If, however, there are only twenty staff in total, full- and part-timers, then such analysis will tell you little or even nothing.

However, the overall purpose of human resource planning will remain the same: to identify for the future how the company will need to use personnel management functions to meet the human resource requirements of the operation.

Methodologies

Figure 6.2 shows how the human resource plan is put together. The various supply and demand criteria will be combined to create an overall policy or plan for the establishment.

1 *Internal supply*: simply the ability of the existing staff to meet the demands of the future. To determine this we first need to examine the usage and skills of the workforce, the internal market. This can be achieved by the use of performance appraisal, training needs analysis or simple managerial judgement.

2 *Future internal supply*: how is the supply likely to change in the future? One change might be that our staff become more skilled as the company trains and develop them. Another may be that they become lazy or dissatisfied as the job is perceived to become too easy or boring. However, the main change will be in whom are actually working for us in the future. How

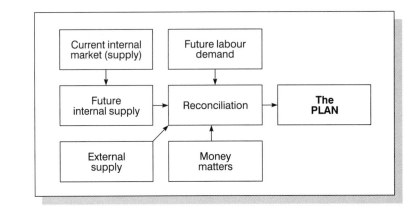

Figure 6.2
Human resource planning
process

many of our current staff will leave us and have to be replaced? This leakage from the organization is termed turnover and needs to be monitored and reduced.

3 *Turnover*: the turnover of staff can be calculated using one of the following formulas.

Turnover index:

$$\frac{\text{No. of staff leaving this year}}{\text{Average no. of staff}} \times 100 \qquad (6.1)$$

e.g. $\dfrac{6}{30} \times 100 = 20\%$

Stability index:

$$\frac{\text{No. of staff with 1 or more years service}}{\text{No. of staff 1 year ago}} \times 100 \qquad (6.2)$$

e.g. $\dfrac{27}{30} \times 100 = 90\%$

The turnover index gives the percentage of leavers and the stability index the percentage of employees who have stayed past their initial year. Both are useful indicators of whether there are problems with turnover but are very basic in the data they supply. They do not take account of such staff as temporary workers, vacational workers or fixed contract staff. Zero turnover is impossible to achieve as events such as retirement, illness or a move away from the area will all cause people to change employment. However, overtly high levels of turnover will indicate levels of dissatisfaction of staff and may lead to higher recruitment, selection and training costs. Monitoring of the reasons for leaving an establishment may indicate to us how the company can rectify the problems. Such monitoring may take the form of exit interviews or questionnaires.

4 *External supply*: this involves the analysis of the labour market at a local or national level. The national level will be important for large companies seeking particularly to attract trainee or assistant management for national expansion. The local analysis will be by managers seeking to identify, for example, sources of recruitment, the competition's methodologies and pay schemes, and the potential pool of labour available to recruit from. Information for this judgemental analysis may be available from the statistics office, census data and local jobcentres, or via professional or craft associations. Comparisons on pay and pay rates may well be an important predictor as to whether or not the organization is going to be able to recruit.

5 *Future demand*: based on the objectives and strategies of the organization, it should be able to determine how much and in what ways the business needs to change its labour force. However, increases in sales or production capacity do not necessarily mean using more staff. The use of new systems, equipment or efficiency methods may allow fairly major expansion of trade without increasing staff numbers.

6 *Reconciliation*: once the business has analysed the data from both a supply and demand perspective, the business then has to formulate HR plans based upon the analyses. This planning may involve the whole range of HRM functions including those based on job design. The reactions of the management will depend on the outcome of the analysis, at both a tactical short-term and strategic long-term level (Table 6.1).

7 *Money matters*: the plans and responses to supply and demand constraints all need to be viewed in the light of the budgets available for action. Given that many of the above processes involve expenditure it may require the adaptation of perfect solutions to meet fiscal strictures.

8 *The plan*: the human resource plan will involve the processes of recruitment, selection, training and payroll administration. However, before we move on to those processes in detail, it should be noted that within the process of analysis the business would derive information on the workers in terms of what they do and when they do it. This can be further examined and presented using job analysis to provide detailed information for the recruitment and selection processes.

Outcome of analysis	Tactical responses	Strategic responses
Demand for staff exceeds supply of staff in numerical terms	Do nothing	Seek new sources for recruitment
	Allow hiring standards to fall	Use recruitment agency
	Allow greater overtime	Form links with local colleges and universities
	Use casual staff	
	Raise comparative pay	Link to job centre and other providers of employment
		Seek new media for recruitment
		Redesign reward system
Demand exceeds supply in skill terms	Let quality fall	Develop existing staff to meet quality requirements
	Deskill the job	
	Subcontract work to agencies	Redesign product or service
Supply exceeds demand in numerical terms	Make staff redundant	Boost demand through selling and marketing activities
	Redeploy staff to other branches or areas	
		Develop new products or service area to absorb staff
	Freeze all recruitment	
Supply exceeds demand in skill terms	Allow staff to become bored and leave	Raise quality thresholds to absorb skills.
		Give more responsibility to skilled staff
	Job rotation and enhancement	Review recruitment and selection criteria

Table 6.1 Tactical and strategic responses to human resource plans

Job analysis and person specifications

One of the most important outcomes of the plan is the likelihood that the business may have to recruit new employees in the future. To do this the business must establish what sort of person is required and what the business wants them to do. The business could use some simple methods of analysis or get really serious and do it scientifically using full work study or extrapolation of past data.

Most licensed house managers will rely on simple techniques to determine what their staff actually does. These techniques include observation, self-analysis, manager's experience, past records or simple work-study.

1 Work study in itself is a very complex and scientific process of identifying the tasks carried out by an employee, the frequency,

time taken and slack time when the employee is waiting for something else to happen. It is more useful in production industries and should really be carried out by professionals in the field.

2 Observation or self-analysis are much easier to carry out as they involve fairly simple skills. The manager can observe their employees at work, note the tasks they complete in a normal work cycle, which would lead to a list of tasks. By asking the employee to list all the jobs they do, and how often they do them, you again will obtain a list of tasks and will also obtain an idea of the frequency of the jobs. The problems with these methods in a small-scale operation are minor and could be ignored but on a larger scale may cause problems because both are very subjective methods and are made inaccurate very easily. If the manager is watching the employees, the employees will change their behaviour just because the manager is watching (the Hawthorne effect – Elton Mayo in Mullins, 1999). This means that they may do different tasks or even use different methods while being watched. Self-analysis may also be inaccurate due to the fact that the employee may deliberately give inflated status or frequency to tasks, possibly as means of soliciting reward or avoiding punishment.

3 Past records are an excellent source of information on the jobs carried out by employees, but not all establishments will have them. The process would involve updating existing analyses rather than starting from scratch.

4 The final method is the simplest and the most commonly used, that of managers themselves determining an employee's task load merely through their own knowledge. This process will again involve the production of a list of tasks, their frequency and standards required. It will of course also be based on what the manager requires the perfect jobholder to have or do, but may be a reasonable method for use in independent or small operations. Most large-scale and company-owned operations would have already defined a list of the tasks required of different job holders.

Job description

One of the basic outcomes from the process of job analysis is the job description (another is the person specification), which in its simplest form is merely a list of tasks and duties to be performed by an employee or a number of employees in an operation.

A straightforward job description will not only assist in the formation of a good recruitment and selection process but will also be used for appraisal and pay analysis. It should contain the information listed in Table 6.2.

Location: both the name of the establishment and the physical location, e.g., bar, restaurant etc.	**Responsibilities:** for physical and financial resources
Movement required: does the job involve travelling or is it located in one place	**Special circumstances**: including special attributes or skills, shifts, weekend work, late hours etc.
Job title: may assist in defining the job. e.g. bar person, waiting staff, chef, kitchen assistant, etc.	**Superior:** the employee's line manager or supervisor. Who is responsible for them?
Job grade: only applicable in larger organizations and will define pay rate and responsibilities	**Subordinates:** for whom is the employee responsible?
Purpose of the job: a detailed statement of what the job entails. The complexity of the purpose will depend on the size of the establishment and the responsibilities of the job	**Main tasks:** a list of the tasks one would carry out in the job. These would be delineated in terms of frequency and importance

Table 6.2 Job description areas

The type and form of the job description can vary enormously in length, detail or format. It may contain a great deal of quantitative or qualitative data, however, most job descriptions are narrative in format with very little use of scientific terminology.

Problems with job descriptions lie in three areas:

1 Reliability – do they reflect what the job is or just what you would like it to be?

2 Appropriateness of descriptions – are they out of date immediately due to evolutionary nature of work?

3 Purposes served by job descriptions – are they just a recruitment tool or does the organization use them elsewhere in the HR function?

Such problems may cause problems for a manager in terms of what is placed in the descriptions and how long they remain valid but are useful in providing information for both applicant and employer.

Person specification

These define the qualifications, experience and personal qualities required of the jobholder, and will include physical conditions, unusual hours or travelling away from home. These are derived from the job analysis processes and should be closely defined.

The danger is overspecification of needs; these may put off candidates or create unhappiness with new job holders whose abilities are underused.

These specifications can be delineated under two different systems. Rodger's seven-point and Fraser's fivefold systems (see Table 6.3). The two systems have been instrumental in shaping person specification for many years.

Lewis (1985) further suggests that these criteria can be further delineated into:

- *organizational*: these characteristics would be those of commitment, timekeeping, honesty and stability

- *functional*: psychomotor skills, dexterity, customer focus, numerical ability and technological awareness

- *individual*: behaviours required of the job holder including calmness, teamwork, communicator, etc.

Seven-point	Fivefold
1 *Physical:* health, physique, appearance, bearing, speech	1 *Impact* on others, general demeanour, appearance, speech
2 *Attainments:* academic attainments, training received, experience	2 *Qualifications:* education, training, work experience
3 *Intelligence:* general intelligence, and the means of assessing these abilities, i.e., numerical ability	3 *Innate abilities:* mental alertness, aptitude for learning
4 *Special aptitudes:* special skills, manual, mechanical, verbal, etc.	4 *Motivation:* consistency, persistency, ability to achieve goals
5 *Disposition:* personality characteristics needed, i.e., self-reliance, drive, energy and initiative.	5 *Adjustment:* stability, reactions to stress, relationships with others
6 *Interests:* personal interests that may impact on job, e.g., social, manual, appreciation of wines.	
7 *Special circumstances:* personal and domestic circumstances that are job related.	

Table 6.3 Person specifications

Attracting candidates to the job: the recruitment process

The processes of recruitment can be encapsulated in Figure 6.3. The answers to the questions in Figure 6.3 are:

1 Does the job actually need somebody in it, can you spread the work between the remaining staff? If you can without undue stress or loss of quality this should be done. Can you replace the person's function within machines or technology? If so then consider that process. (See Chapter 7.)

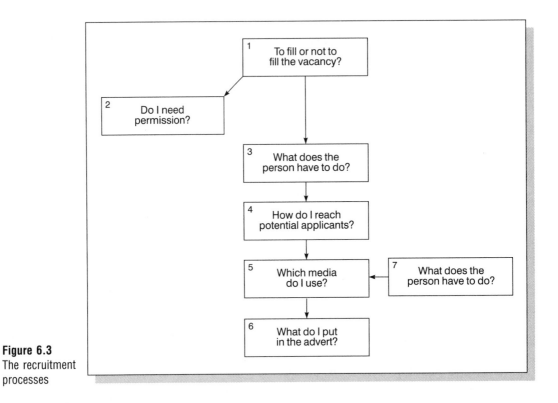

Figure 6.3
The recruitment
processes

2 Many organizations require permission from area or district management before recruiting. An employment requisition is normally issued and authorization given. Independent or smaller operations may not require this.

3 The information has already been prepared in the job description and person specification. These should be prepared for distribution to candidates and for use in selection.

4 What recruitment sources are available. Table 6.4 lists the main sources we could use for recruitment, however, the benefits and drawbacks for each should be considered. Whichever source is used the manager must be sure that the process is cost-effective and not disproportional to the importance or contribution the employee has in the outlet.

Advertising

This is the most simple and straightforward way of attracting candidates, but it can be expensive and the use of advertising must be closely examined to ensure it is economically valid. The objectives of an advertisement should be to:

- attract attention
- create and maintain interest
- stimulate action.

Sources	Advantages	Disadvantages
Internal	Provides promotional opportunities for existing staff	Always promoting from within may cause resentment within a team
	You already know all about the staff and can make simple decisions	New ideas and innovation may not enter the organization
	The process is cheap and simple	Might be overly subjective
External advertisement	Allows access to a wide range of potential applicants	Even local advertising might be expensive
	Can attract enough applicant to fill multiple vacancies	Quality of advert needs to meet image of outlet
		Might attract a vast range of applicants many of whom are unsuitable
Employment agencies	*Job centres*	*Job centres*
	Free use of space for both recruitment and interviewing	Might not reach skilled workers wishing to change jobs
	Reach those available for work immediately	Does not always filter totally unsuitable candidates
	Commercial agencies	*Commercial agencies*
	Skill and expertise in recruitment	Extremely expensive, not suitable for most posts below management
	Takes all responsibility for the process once specifications drawn up	Require detailed specifications
Education and training establishments	Colleges and universities would be able to provide skilled employees at all levels	Would seek jobs to match their talents and expectations
	Might also provide pool of casual labour	Possibly overqualified to fulfil immediate role and would require the chance of progression quickly
	Free services offered by many establishments	
Employment training schemes	Provides a cost-effective worker supported by training agency	Many are under 18 and not available to work in alcohol-based areas
	Would provide trial period before full employment	
	Would help focus training and development as required by the terms of the scheme	
Other external sources	Ex-service personnel, skilled and experienced, helped by armed service in terms of resettlement periods	May have a disciplined background out of step with the establishment
	Student placements, for fixed periods of time	Only limited time before you have to replace them but may suit specific instances
	Specialist agencies in settling and resettling individuals in society, this may include rehabilitation or underrepresented people in employment	May require special conditions but many are supported by funding

Table 6.4 Recruitment sources

To achieve these objectives six things need to be done:

1 Analyse requirement.

2 Decide who does what.

3 Write the copy.

4 Design the advertisement..

5 Plan media.

6 Evaluate response in the following areas:
   (a) initial enquiries
   (b) number of candidates at each stage of recruitment and selection
   (c) number of candidates recruited
   (d) number of candidates retained for 6 months.

Sorting and selecting

Sifting applications

Assuming that the vacancy has been advertised and that a number of replies have been received, the typical sequence of steps is as follows:

1 List the applicants on a control sheet giving the name, source, address and the dates of the following actions: acknowledgement, interview, final letter and start date.

2 Send a standard acknowledgement letter to each candidate. (Not standard practice in all establishments but a very good public relations exercise.)

3 Compare each applicant against the criteria set within the person specification. Sort into three categories: possible, marginal and unsuitable.

4 Scrutinize the possible and draw up a short list. This scrutiny should be carried out in conjunction with supervisors or other line managers.

5 Invite candidates for interview.

6 Write to marginal applicants if you wish to keep them as the reserve. Write to unsuitable thanking them for their application.

Application form

The application form is a very useful tool in recruitment but its design must be carefully considered. The following are the main considerations in this area:

1 Ask only for relevant and pertinent information.

2 Allow the candidate to answer fully the questions by providing enough space in which to enter details.

Staff Application Form Please complete all parts of the form and give it to the branch manager. Please complete the form in black ink and use block capitals. The information in the form will be used as part of the selection procedure for the job. All information provided is confidential and no reference to your previous or present employers will be made without prior permission.

Job Applied for	Branch name
Personal details Family Name	First Name(s)
Address Post Code………………………………………..	Telephone Number…………………………… Email Address………………………………….

How did you about learn of this vacancy?……………………………….…………………

Date of birth…………	Age………………..	Are you a registered disabled person YES/NO If yes registration Number……………………

Ethnic Origin……………………………………..
(Please refer to attached list) This information is for monitoring purposes only and will not be used as a selection criteria)

Education

School attended	Dates	Exams Passed	Grades	Dates
College/ university attended	Dates	Exams Passed	Grades	Dates

Employment History

Present Employer	Job title
Present Salary/Wage Rate	Starting date

Previous Employment (starting with the job previous to your present position).

Employer	Position	From	Until	Reason for leaving

Medical History Please outline any medical issues we need to be aware of.

Please give any further information which you think should be taken into account in considering your application. You may wish to include professional, recreational and other activities here.

When would you be able to take up your new appointment?

Please give the name of one personal referee to whom we may address a request for a personal reference apart from your present employer.

Signature……………………………..   Date

Received	Interview?	Appoint?	Start date?	Reject?

Figure 6.4 Example application form. (Space has been truncated for illustrative purposes only)

3 Allow the candidate to provide additional information that they believe may help their application.

4 Specify how the form is to be filled in, i.e., colour of ink, handwritten, etc.

5 Allow space for the job they are applying for to be entered.

6 The questions are easy to answer and unambiguous.

7 Ensure details of previous work experience are requested.

For many jobs a simple application form will suffice, however, particularly for skilled and managerial positions, you may wish to use a more complex process. The following might be used:

- curriculum vitae (CV): all the details of a person's life drawn up by the candidate

- letters of application: a free-form version of the application form with the details required delineated by the manager.

Interviewing arrangements

There are several styles of interview available depending on the type of job and the organization's requirements, but the following points are valid for all interviews:

1 *Comfort*: uncomfortable candidates may not show themselves off well. Remember they may be nervous.

2 *Peace and time*: the interview will not be a good one if you are constantly interrupted or have only limited time in which to do it. Allow enough time to complete each interview.

3 *Ease*: put the candidate at his or her ease as soon as possible. Interviewers will receive fuller and more honest answers from people they gain a rapport with.

4 *Notes*: always take note of the applicant's answer and write them down. Listening is the most important skill in interviewing; listen to what is said, and perhaps what is not said, by the applicant.

5 *Open questions*: always ask open questions, which require a fuller answer than 'yes' or 'no'. Allow the applicant to answer fully the question and to show off their full range of skills and attributes.

6 *Probe*: never be afraid to gain more detail on an applicant's answer. Probe as to why they said or did things.

7 *Equality*: give every candidate an equal chance. Try not to judge too early in the interview. Use an interview plan with a series of planned areas to cover rather than a fixed script.

8 *Control*: keep control of the interview, do not let the candidate run away with the process.

9 *Finish*: always finish the interview definitely. Inform the candidate of the next stage in the process, and when they will receive the results of the interview. Do not promise the job to a candidate until all candidates have been seen.

Types of interview

The individual or one-to-one interview is the most common type used. Table 6.5 shows the advantages and disadvantages of this type and of the other types of interview.

It may be necessary to carry out more than one interview with each candidate to whittle down the potential job holders further, to allow for further skills-based assessment or to ensure equality. However, in most positions the single one-to-one process is used. The recruitment of managers and graduate trainees may involve further testing (see below) and for skilled practitioners (e.g., chefs) practical tests *in situ* may be needed.

	Advantages	Disadvantages
Individual interviews (one candidate one interviewer)	Simple to organize and control Easy to build a rapport with candidate Decision-making simpler	Decision based on one interviewer's judgement only (bias) Successful outcome based solely on skill of interviewer
Panel interviews (one candidate more than one interviewer)	Decision based on more than one person's skill Specialist questions from panel members possible Decision less likely to be biased	Compromise candidate may be selected due to disagreement among panel (dependent on panel size) More difficult to organize and build rapport (size does matter) Large panel may intimidate candidate
Group selection (more than one candidate; group assessed on abilities such as verbal skills, group interaction, and leadership)	Can demonstrate a range of abilities not seen in other forms Can be used in conjunction with individual interviews or as first interview to gain wider view of candidate's abilities	Strong members of group may dominate Needs a high-order skill to organize and assess properly Time-consuming

Table 6.5 Interview types

Psychological and psychometric testing

Although the interview is a well tried and tested means of selection, there has in the 1990s been a great deal of use of testing as a means of bringing greater objectivity and validity to the selection function. The basic concept behind testing is that test scores relate or correlate to job performance.

Types of test

1 Aptitude test used to measure innate ability of candidate. (Not often used outside armed forces or as part of careers advice.)

2 Intelligence test measuring a candidate's intellectual capacity in areas such as numerical, verbal and oral skills, perceptual speed.

3 Trainability used to measure the learning speed and skills of candidates.

4 Attainment tests based on vocational psychomotor skills such as cooking, sommelier or cellar management.

5 Personality tests attempt to define an individual's personality traits and determine whether candidate's personality profile meets job requirements.

Where tests are used

Tests are used for differing purposes by companies but are more often used for senior positions rather than operative.

Job grade	%
Administration	40
Secretarial	37
Manual	20
Graduates	90
Junior management	70
Middle management	80
Senior management	70

Source: Shackleton and Newell, 1991.

Table 6.6
Use of tests

Is testing a good idea?

Any method of testing is useful if it fulfils certain basic criteria. The first criterion is validity, does it actually measure that which we want to measure? Then reliability, does it reproduce the same results every time? Ease of use and interpretation, can the test be carried out simply and can the results be easily understood? Context of test, do the results actually indicate success or failure in the job? If the answer to all these questions is 'yes' then we should use the tests. However there are several recognized problems associated with some tests:

1 *Correlation*: correlation between testing and job performance is low, in some even very low.

2 *Time*: the tests take time and effort to arrange and interpret.

3 *Changes*: jobs and people change over time. A test result today may not reflect skills or abilities needed to carry out the future role.

4 *Bias and pressure*: some tests are biased against some groups of people. They also put abnormal pressure on the testee, which would not give a true picture of abilities.

The use of tests should be limited to that of support to other methods of selection rather than a pure method of selection. They should only be used by trained personnel.

Evaluation and validation of recruitment and selection

The proof of the pudding is said to be in the eating of it. The proof required of recruitment and selection procedures lies in the long-term success of the personnel recruited to the establishment. The management of any licensed house must attempt to review each part of the process in terms of whether it has met the objectives set for it. The job description and specification should be analysed in terms of their use for the interviewer but also as to whether it supplied the correct information to the successful candidate. Does the specification actually match the job the person is doing? If it does not this part of the process needs to be reviewed. The external advertising needs to be evaluated in terms of both quantity and quality of respondents. Which media brought in the most candidates and those who most closely met our requirements. Those that had poor responses should be assessed in terms of the advert itself, its size, wording and placement in the media. The interviewing process should also be assessed via the successful candidates for the most part, to identify successful and weak areas.

Having said this it should be observed that it might be a long time before we can determine whether or not we have made the right selection and recruitment decision, as it takes time for the employee to reach their potential. That potential can only be achieved if we successfully train and develop the job holder. Once we have the people we think we need, we must mould them into an effective workforce.

Training and learning

The aims of training are to:

- shorten learning time so that new recruits reach their peak of efficiency as quickly and economically as possible
- improve the performance of existing employees
- help people to develop themselves to their maximum potential so as to aid in job satisfaction and the meeting of the organization's need for future supervisors, managers and higher-grade workers.

Systematic training

Systematic training is the process of identifying and implementing a process of development that meets both organizational and individual goals (see Figure 6.5).

However, in order to successfully implement systematic training the manager should have an understanding of how and why people learn effectively.

Learning theory

Learning theory provides the background to training, emphasizing the basic components of how to get people to learn what you want them to learn, at the level you want them to learn, for the length of time you have to spend on it.

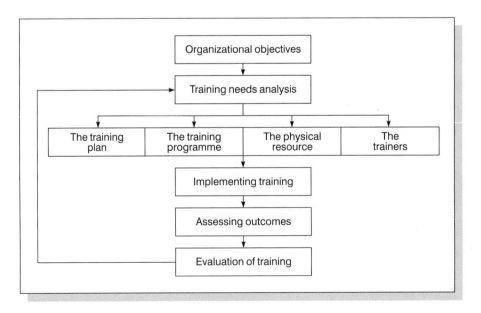

Figure 6.5
Systematic training

Conditions for achieving effective learning:

1 *Motivation*: the learner needs to have some reason to learn, a motivation to become more skilful or knowledgeable. Linking training to promotion, pay or other motivational areas, i.e., safety, security would provide that impetus.

2 *Standards*: the learner needs to have standards defined for the outcome of the training, to know when they have completed it and what standards they have reached – the goalposts.

3 *Guidance*: in order to reach the set standards learners need guidance. The role of trainer, mentor, coach, etc., is vital here in both guiding the learner and providing feedback on progress to trainee and manager.

4 *Satisfaction*: the learner must gain something from the training itself. In most instances intrinsic satisfaction of knowing new things and having new skills may suffice. However, the use of extrinsic rewards such as badges, certificates, award ceremonies and promotional prospects will also help considerably in providing motivation and satisfaction.

5 *Activity*: the learner should be involved actively in the learning process. The school-room scenario may alienate some learners. Active participation, audiovisual and technology use, role-play and practice will not only allow the learner to develop skills and knowledge but will also maintain the learner's interest.

6 *Techniques*: the techniques used to train should be applicable to the skill being developed. Teaching someone how to clean beer lines in theory is useful, but by demonstrating it and allowing the learner to participate will considerably enhance the learning.

7 *Variation*: a variety of different techniques should be used wherever possible not only to enhance learning, but also to provide further interest within the trainee.

8 *Time*: adequate time should be allocated to the learning process not only in terms of ensuring that the information or skills are received by the learner, but also in ensuring that the learner has time to practise the skills before they use them in earnest.

9 *Reinforcement*: reinforcing learning is the process of checking whether the learner can actually use the skills and knowledge they have gained. Practice, drills, revision sessions and allowing the learner to use skills on the public under supervision will allow reinforcement and provide evidence to the trainer that learning has taken place.

10 *Differences*: trainer must recognize that different people learn in very different ways. Some may rebel against the classroom-type learning but respond to small group or individual practical training. People learn at different rates, depending on their perceptual speeds. Trainers must pace their sessions to suit both the needs of the trainee and the complexity of the skills.

Note: Learning curve: although many skills can be taught and learnt in a short space of time, a wide range of skills will take time to build. People learn at a particular rate described as a learning curve. The greater the steepness of that curve the greater the ability of the learner to actually absorb information.

Behaviour modelling

Some of the most difficult areas of skills to develop in trainees are behavioural ones, those involved in such areas as customer skills, complaint management and group interaction. One of the most effective ways of achieving these behaviours in trainees is to use the process of behaviour modelling. This involves the trainee observing correct behaviours in context and being shown how to adopt them. The use of videos and computer-based interactive learning may be of assistance in this area but the most successful method is in shadowing and mentoring. The trainee is attached to a skilled employee who then demonstrates and allows the trainee to practise his or her skills under the employee's guidance. The role of careful selection of employees is key here with only those candidates who show an ability to adopt correct behaviours being taken into the organization.

Identification of training needs

Training needs are not just those of any particular individual but also those of the group, department and organization as a whole. Training is quite often carried out only for the sake of training: 'It's good for us.' With that sort of attitude training is less than useless. To be effective there must be specific aims to training, to fulfil gaps in the organization's, the group's or the individual's skills profile.

One of the simplest forms of identifying areas that require the use of training is the gap analysis approach.

Gap analysis • • •

This involves the manager in identifying problematic areas (gaps) in the organization and then how training can close those gaps (Figure 6.6). The gaps may not all be due to training or even human resource problems but by carrying out such an analysis the manager will identify causes and potential solutions.

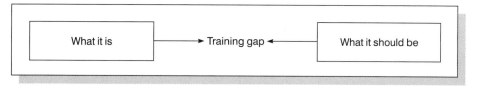

Figure 6.6 Training gap

The sum of individual and group needs will indicate the corporate needs, however there may be some superordinate needs that will be defined by the organization itself. These will be linked either to strategic issues or those based on compliance with legislative processes.

Methods of identifying gaps

The methods listed in Table 6.7 are ways in which the manager of any licensed house may identify problem areas.

Table 6.7
Sources of training gap analysis information

Analysis of business plan	Human resource planning processes
Job analysis	Job description
Job specifications	Complaints
Questionnaires	Performance appraisal
Financial results	Wastage
Exit interviews	Customer comments

Of these the most important are those based on the employee feedback, appraisal process and customer-based comments and complaints.

Preparing training plans

The training plan will come from the summary of training needs at individual group and organizational levels. The summary of training needs should establish the main areas and priorities for training. The summary should be supported by the detailed training specifications for each occupation. The overall summary should set out for each category of employee:

- numbers to be involved
- new employees expected as part of the HR planning process
- level of pre-training of both expected and existing staff
- methods necessary to fulfil training needs
- approximate cost of programme.

Training policies

It may seem strange to set policies at this stage but the policy can only be designed once the total plan has been determined. The policy would delineate the priorities that are being assigned to the total plan. The highest priorities would be health and safety, hygiene and fire training, with lower-priority work being assigned until the budget is exhausted. Those needs that were very individual in nature would either be assigned to the next budget period or only partly funded.

Where should training take place?

There are a number of choices in this area (see Table 6.8).

Method	Advantages	Disadvantages
In-house on the job (at the point of work)	Useful for skills and knowledge related directly to work, i.e., practical skills	Requires skilled trainer
	Involves small group or individual training so can be paced to suit learners	Might be carried out in front of customers or colleagues causing embarrassment
	Does not remove learner or trainer from work environment	Difficult to use for complex tasks or knowledge
	Is reasonably low in cost	
	Assessment of skills and feedback immediate	
In-house off the job (still on the premises but away from the place of work)	Can be used to pass information and knowledge to larger numbers of staff	Does remove trainer and larger numbers of trainees from work place
	By using external resources (videos, etc.) can be used to cover specific areas	Might require specialist equipment or facilities
	Removal from work area is just for the length of the session	Pace may be a problem
	Useful in demonstrating and practising complex skills	Might not be immediately applicable to all participants
	Feedback and assessment possible	Might not reflect the reality of the outlet
External training	Provides up-to-date practices and skills	Might be very expensive
	Would involve trainees in interaction with others and the movement of best practice into the outlet	Skills would be transferable and opens possibility of staff being poached by other employers
	Might provide accredited learning for training	The range of skills and knowledge may not be instantly applicable to the trainee. If those skills are not used the training is not effective
	Provide training not available within the organization	
	Might be funded by external agencies	

Table 6.8 Training places

Training techniques

The range of techniques available to the trainer is vast, from simple demonstration and practice to state-of-the art computer-based techniques. They are listed in generic areas in Table 6.9. The choice of which technique to use is based on the skills or knowledge required, the skill of the trainer and the resources available to the organization. Choosing the right technique is vital and the success or failure of the entire process may be dependent on the choice.

Table 6.9
Training techniques

Show and tell	Lectures, demonstrations, video films, books and handbooks, standards manuals.
Show and use	Coaching, mentoring, tutorials, seminars, discussion groups, computer-based learning.
Trainee does it	Books and handbooks, practice, simulations, role-play.

Resources

The training resources available will depend on how much money is available from the training budget. This in turn is determined by the profitability of the organization and senior management's and directors' attitudes towards training. The two main types of resources are the tools or technology for training, i.e., physical resources, and the human resources available to be trained.

Human resources

This refers to the trainers who are going to carry out the training itself. The trainers need to be trained in how to train. Some people are natural trainers but most must have their innate talents honed. The trainer needs to know how to demonstrate a skill, how to watch a trainee attempt the skill, without interfering, and give feedback and assessment to the trainee. A range of trainers within an organization will ensure that all possible skill areas are covered and that the load is evenly spread among the senior staff.

Physical resources

These resources are split into:

- *static*: blackboards, books, paper, overhead projectors (OHPs), slides

- *dynamic*: radio, television, video, films, tapes

- *interactive*: computers, simulators, interactive video.

The wider the range of resources available to train, the wider the range of techniques used and, hence, the more effective they will be.

Evaluation of training

This area of the training cycle is the one most often neglected or only superficially carried out. In fact it is the most important part of the whole process while also being one of the simplest.

Evaluation of the effects of training is the process of determining the effect that the training itself has had upon the trainee. In some types of training, e.g., those concerned with reducing wastage or improving productivity, the evaluation is very easy to carry out because the quantitative data provided for other organizational uses will quickly indicate whether or not training has helped. More nebulous benefits may be more difficult to assess.

The most common way used to try and do this is the post-course questionnaire asking for the trainees' reaction to the course. However, the trainees may be unlikely to respond accurately to vague questions about their experience and in many cases the removal from the work environment may have been seen as a positive outcome and the trainee unlikely to endanger the chance to do it again in the future. Torrington and Hall (1998) advocate the expectation versus outcome evaluation, i.e., pre-training and post-training questionnaires, to analyse whether or not expectations have been met.

Note: What are we expecting from the training? In trying to evaluate our training we should always do so in terms of the objectives we have set ourselves. We may not always achieve all objectives but through evaluation and then modification of the training process we will improve both performance and training skills.

Induction training

Definition: 'Arrangements made to familiarise the new employee with the working organization, welfare and safety matters, general conditions of work, and the work of the department in which they are to be employed' (Department of Employment, 1971).

Why induct? The reasons are straightforward. The new entrant into the organization faces two challenges. The first is developing the required skills to meet the job requirements and can be overcome by using a systematic training process. The second is integrating himself or herself into the organization at a personal level. The process of integration or non-integration is known as the induction crisis. If the new employee is accepted into the working group quickly and is able to handle the stresses and strains that the job brings, then they are less likely to leave during the first few weeks of employment. One of the most effective means of overcoming this crisis is by carrying out an induction programme. To introduce the organization to new employees and the employees to the organization, to show them where they fit in, where they work, with whom they work and that they are valued members of the team.

What is in an induction programme?

The programme should cover all the aspects in Table 6.10 but are not limited only to these areas. The most important part of the process is actually assessing how the employee has integrated and what remedial action needs to take place to complete the process.

Personnel policies	The way in which they will be managed, monitored and feedback given to them
Terms and conditions	The basis of their relationship to the organization. Their rewards and incentives, their contracted terms
Employee benefits	What else they can expect from their employment
Physical resources	Where everything is, from cloakroom to manager's office, cleaner's cupboard to spirit stores, giving them the ability to navigate around the building
Nature of work	What is expected of them. Further details or a repeat of the job description
The supervisor/ manager	Who their boss or line manager is
Rules and regulations	The rules and regulations covering their work, especially in term of fire, hygiene and health and safety
Relationships	Who they are in charge of, the people they work with, names and faces of their colleagues
The job itself	Shown in a practical sense how to do things
Follow up	Are the new employees happy? Do they have the information they require? Are they working safely and properly?

Source: After Pigors and Myers, 1977.

Table 6.10
Induction areas

Teamwork and teams

One of the most important aspects of people at work is the way in which they work together, whether in small or large groups. The bar, food service, food production, administration or even management teams, all must work with each other and with other groups to make the organization a success. No single team can function without the other; each must communicate and co-operate with the others. However, the number of conflicts that exist within even a small pub are legion: 'John won't talk to Sandra', 'Chef never talks to anybody' or 'The boss never tells us anything' are familiar stories for most people.

So the questions arise; what is a team? Why do these problems occur? How to get over these problems? How can we get people to work together? The answers are not simple or straightforward because they deal with the most complex and difficult things on this planet – *people*.

The rest of this chapter has dealt with the operational methodology, the systems and procedures for bringing together a group of people to fulfil the needs of the business, but if they cannot work together then all else is for naught.

What is a team?

A team is a very special group of people, they have to work together otherwise they fail. They must voluntarily work together, they are highly dependent upon each other, and their individual efforts as a team member determine the team success. The formation and maintenance of work teams is a vital ingredient of success for any managers. Team behaviours and norms such as speed of work, responsibility for jobs and authority within the group have to monitored and controlled by the manager. A team may hide less able workers and support them, and in time improve that worker. People who are unable or unwilling to work in teams should not be selected or should be moved to areas where they can work on their own.

Performance management and individual performance

It has been the case in the past that most performance reviews have centred on the relationship between work and reward, with performance related to the interaction between ability and motivation. However, it is now more common to perceive improved performance as the interaction between performance goals, standards, appropriate resources, guidance and support.

If this is true then managers and employee must engage the process of recognizing these factors within work and plan for their implementation. This process is known as performance management.

The performance cycle

This cycle encapsulates the process required for the enhancement of performance (Figure 6.7).

For the unit manager the three aspects of Figure 6.7 are interlinked. *Planning performance* in terms of setting standards and practices is vital to ensure all the manager's staff know what they have to do and how to do it. In *supporting performance* the manager is providing the training to facilitate the planned performance. In *reviewing performance* the manager enters into the area of performance appraisal.

Performance appraisal

Appraisal is the formalization of the review part of the performance cycle. Appraisal done badly is a waste of time for everyone involved; appraisal done well can improve motivation

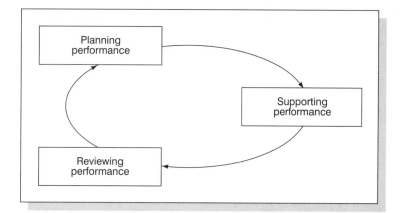

Figure 6.7
The performance cycle
Source: Torrington and Hall
(1998).

and performance for both appraise and appraiser, and can greatly assist both individual development and organizational planning.

What is appraisal

'Appraisal', 'performance assessment', 'performance evaluation', 'individual assessment', 'job appraisal' are common titles referring to the same basic process. The terminology normally indicates the emphasis placed on the process. However described, the process can fit one of two patterns:

1 *Informal*: motivational, recognition, praise, correction, training, short term, ad hoc.

2 *Formal*: Interviews, questionnaires, periodic, long term, linked to strategy, pay or discipline.

The uses of appraisal

The results of appraisal are often used for a number of differing purposes, which quite often lead to conflict between them. This conflict lies in the fact that the purpose of each is different. For example in reviewing past performance we are setting out to locate areas of weakness and suggest means to overcome them; if we are setting pay levels from appraisal then the last thing the employees wants is for the mistakes of the past to be held against them. Thus employees are less likely to assist in the process if the process damages them rather than assists them.

Uses	Blue collar	White collar	Management
1 Set performance objectives	35	125	164
2 Assess past performance	72	189	208
3 Improve current performance	77	197	214
4 Assess training needs	65	200	215
5 Assess increases to pay	35	92	104
6 Assess future potential	63	175	200
7 Assist in career planning	35	139	168
8 Others	6	11	9

Note: sample size 350 companies; figures indicate number of times the use was mentioned.
Source Torrington and Hall, 2nd edn: 142)

Table 6.11 Appraisal usage

Who is appraised and who appraises?

Table 6.12
Level of appraisal usage

Manual unskilled	92	Manual skilled and technical	119
Clerical/secretarial	189	Supervisory	215
Middle management	251	Senior management	229

Source: Torrington and Hall, 2nd edn.

The appraiser ● ● ●

The decision as to who carries out the appraisal is important for overall success in the process. It involves the difficult task of gaining objective judgements of the employee rather than subjective decisions based in bias. Each choice in this area has a positive side but also difficult negatives:

1 *Superior appraisal*: by the line manager of the employee. Useful in that the supervisor knows the individual, their work and the standards required. Problematical in that personal feeling may easily enter the process either positively or negatively. Too close?

2 *Superior's superior appraisal*: using a manager one level up from the line manager. Brings less chance of bias and perhaps better management skills to the process but this manager would not see the individual's entire work, and knowledge may be limited to success and failures. The superior's superior would also have to appraise a large number of employees. Too far away?

3 *Self-appraisal*: allow the employee to do it himself or herself. Logically they are the people who know themselves best but they are also the most subjective. Some employees may not be able to express themselves in appraisal unless given significant guidelines. They would express their own personal development needs clearly. Not able?

4 *Appraisal by peers*: useful information may be gained from this source in terms of how the employee works in a group and communicates, but a strong team ethos may deflect from the objectivity of the peer group.

5 *Appraisal by subordinates*: useful information on management style and communication skills but likely to be subjective and difficult to gain if not anonymous.

Which one to choose? As each method has a major drawback the obvious answer would be, use more than one. Each gives us a particular viewpoint, why not use all of them? The problem there lies in too much information and the time it takes to gather, interpret and use the data. Therefore, in most situations, a combination of self and superior appraisal will suffice. The employee will fill in an appraisal form outlining his or her own strengths and weaknesses, and hopes and aspirations for the future. The superior would also fill in a similar form. This would then be discussed with the superior and an agreed set of assessments noted. Where there is conflict between the two sets of appraisal the superior's superior could rule on the process and would have the opportunity to view all appraisals.

What is appraised?

One of the most important concerns here is the avoidance of personality measures. We are not trying to assess the individual's personality but are trying to gain a clear insight into their achievements and future. There are several ways to approach this:

1 *Behaviourally anchored rating scale (BARS)*: where the employee is rated against a predetermined set of behaviours. These behaviours would be at a standard level for the entire organization and would range from perfect behaviours to non-acceptable on a four-point or six-point scale. Assessment of the behaviours would result in a profile of grades that would identify strengths and weaknesses of the employee.

2 *Behavioural observation scale*: similar to BARS but the scale is developed in terms of the employees in the organization rather than against an absolute scale. It makes the scales more applicable to the organization and over time would show how different people within the outlet are progressing, or not, as the better workers push the top of the scale upwards.

3 *Meeting objectives*: if at each appraisal meeting objectives for improvement are set, then at subsequent meetings the employee can be measured against them. Failure in any objective would be analysed and the reason for it assessed, as would exceeding the objectives. Where the employee is responsible for the performance, then they would be credited or penalized for it. Where external influences or failures were due to lack of resources or training then these could be addressed.

4 *Performance against job description*: might be useful during initial employment but as the job develops over time it would become less and less useful.

5 *Performance against competencies*: measuring against competencies is extremely objective but requires skilled assessment by the appraiser. Failure to meet competencies could be remedied by training or discipline as required.

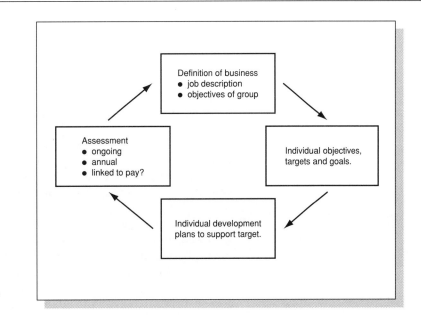

Figure 6.8
The appraisal system
Source: Bevan and Thompson, 1992.

Making appraisal work

No matter which system is used to assess the employee, or the overall purpose of the scheme, there are a number of criteria that must be observed to make appraisal work properly:

1 *Purpose of the system*: must be determined closely by the management of the enterprise. The number of purposes assigned to it should be small as trying to achieve too much from it creates conflict within those purposes. This set of purposes must also be clearly defined for the employees so that they understand why it is being done, what their benefits are from the system or even the consequences of bad appraisals.

2 *Ownership*: although the process may be management driven, the employees must feel that they have a stake in the process, that they can influence the outcome and that the process is fair. If this does not happen then resentment will occur.

3 *Openness and participation*: the openness of the system ensures that it is free from abuse and bias, that the participants have had a fair say and have been listened to.

4 *Appraisal criteria*: the criteria within the system should be such that they are applicable to the staff being appraised and the staff are able to achieve them. If we set criteria for appraisal that the employee has no control over then that appraisal is

useless, e.g., assessing bar staff or the speed of food served in restaurant.

5 *Training:* those carrying out the appraisal, and those being appraised need to be trained in the process itself. They all need to know what to do and how to do it.

6 *Action:* the appraisal must lead to action by the organization whether it be training, work design or discipline, the employee must see something result from the process. It should also be agreed that the employee will also take action.

7 *Review:* once an appraisal is complete that appraisal must be reviewed in terms of the actions decided within it (the action plan). That plan will be reviewed appraised and amended. Often it is the case that appraisals take place once a year and this review is half-yearly, thus giving time for improvement and ensuring that action is taking place.

Payment and reward

Payment, compensation, remuneration, reward – all words signifying the basic concept of giving an employee money or other things of worth for their labour. Whichever term is used the concepts are still the same, however, the type of payment, the amount of payment and the increase in that payment are of prime concern to employers and also to their employees.

The axiom of a fair day's pay for a fair day's work is one which should be seen as a guide to pay but this is not the only consideration.

Employees' expectations

These would be expressed in the following terms:

1 *Purchasing power:* the amount of pay after taxation that the employee can spend. The employee would wish this to increase above the rate of inflation in order for their overall prosperity to increase.

2 *Fairness:* that they are receiving reward for their labours. That the effort that they put into work is actually reflected in what they get out of it.

3 *Rights:* that the reward that they get meets their rights in terms of law and in terms of equity. The organization that is extremely profitable and does not put some of that money into the pocket of its employees would not be seen as equitable.

4 *Relativities*: that the pay in their organization is on a par with that in other organizations in the area. It does not have to be more if there are other benefits but these may be outweighed if the pay is too low.

5 *Recognition*: that the reward they gain is a true reflection of their effort and status.

6 *Composition*: that the composition of the reward is such that they can calculate such things as incentives and bonuses, that overtime is a possibility and is paid accordingly.

Employer objectives

1 *Prestige*: there is prestige in being a good payer and such a name will be seen as a positive marketing and recruitment tool.

2 *Competition*: as pay might be an initial reason for applying to an organization, then reasonable pay levels will act as a positive force. Being perceived as being a higher payer than the competition will make recruitment simpler.

3 *Control*: if there is an element of pay based on incentives, performance or productivity, then this will allow a level of control for the manager.

4 *Motivation and performance*: control over pay may also provide motivation for the employee and hence improve productivity. Motivated employees are also more likely to stay.

5 *Cost*: cost is an extremely important element in pay. The biggest cost in a licensed house is likely to be staff costs. These have to be controlled as a proportion of sales. If the proportion of sales to labour costs is not right then the profits of the business will fall.

What is pay?

Pay is made up of several different elements. The elements have different levels of flexibility and are either under management, legal or contractual control.

Incentives and incentive schemes

Incentive pay was one of the most contentious and absorbing issues to face managers in the 1990s. The search for the concept of the Holy Grail type way of linking the performance of the individual to reward and thereby truly creating the fairest possible system of reward. This system would allow the manager time to concentrate on the planning and strategy of work rather than the supervision of workers as they would be striving on

Title	Types	Features
Basic rate of pay or salary	Basic and non-reducible; level determined by government pay minima and market forces	Salaried workers might only be eligible for these benefits and incentives
Benefits	Benefit schemes: cars, pensions, health insurance, discount schemes, crèche, etc.	Fixed, rarely variable, usually contractual
	Payment in kind; meals, accommodation, free use of facilities	
	Occasional	Fixed, rarely variable
Premia	Contractual	Usually contractual
	Based on added responsibility within the organization; might include bank holiday or difficult work	Variable, irregular
Overtime	For extra hours worked above contracted work; useful to meet short-term shortfall in staff; not recommended as long-term solution	Variable, irregular, mainly contractual
Incentives	Group basis	Variable, irregular
	Individual basis	Mainly contractual based on the performance of individual or organization
Bonuses	Profit allocation	Variable
	Discretionary sum	Irregular
	Base on special occasions or as profit share	Mainly contractual

Table 6.13 Elements of pay

their own, on what Torrington and Hall (1998) describe as 'automatic pilot'.

Incentives and the way in which they are structured delineate the ideas of managers towards their employees. They describe the relationship that exists between them, i.e., the managers believe the way to get better work is through reward. The relationship is further complicated by the use of a whole range of fringe benefits that are seen as a sop to employees rather than as a just reward.

Incentives still proliferate in pay systems with an average level of 15–25 per cent of pay as incentives and 39 per cent of manual workers and 19 per cent of non-manual workers receiving incentives.

Managerial expectations of incentives

The management's expectations of incentive schemes are based on the concepts of motivation, control and cost. The aim is for the incentives to motivate staff to work harder and better for a proportional increase in costs. This increase in performance would allow the manager to both control costs and exert influence on the staff.

Employee expectation of incentives

These expectations are in terms of orientation to work, autonomy and interest. Employee will attempt to earn incentives, whether they are extrinsic or intrinsic, if they perceive a close link between the incentive and what they are doing. Also that they have some ability to affect that incentive (autonomy) and that they are interested in gaining it.

Problems with incentives

Many of the problems with incentives are based on operational inefficiencies – the employees are hindered in gaining reward due to problems outside their control. This is coupled with problems relating to the distance between some incentives and the work itself, e.g., profit sharing would only be given after the company's financial year end perhaps fourteen months after the effort began. Incentives also cause fluctuations in earnings for the employees when they would rather have continuous reward in terms of overall pay levels.

Performance-related pay

Performance-related pay is related to appraisal and therefore directly related to work over a given period. Pay increases or decreases are possible and are sometimes based on the concept of competition or standard distribution of reward. It makes the process individual rather than group and thus, potentially, more acceptable to employees. However, with the potential for abuse and subjectivity within the appraisal scheme, performance-related pay is often viewed as being unfair.

Profit-sharing

Profit-sharing schemes, whether cash or share ownership, have the incentive of rewarding those staff who stay with the business for a long period of time, but the periodicity of the reward does dilute the effect of the reward. Inland Revenue approved schemes (tax exempt) do have the effect of promoting loyalty to the company by ensuring employees themselves also become stakeholders in the enterprise.

Motivation and retention

Throughout this chapter aspects of motivation and retention have been continually referred to. The effect that the management of human resources has upon these factors is enormous. Staff who are carefully selected, inducted, trained and developed, and who have a fair reward, are likely to be both positive contributors to the success of the organization and to stay in that organization. The process involves time, effort and money from the management of an organization but the rewards in terms of profitability and success are enormous.

Equality at work

It must be noted in any discussion on human resources in the licensed trade that equality of opportunity is both a legal and moral necessity. Any practice that does not allow for the integration into the workforce of any group of people is dangerous in terms of both its legality and its public relations contexts. Managers should ensure that their recruitment, selection, training needs analysis, training, appraisal and pay practices are free not only of discrimination, but also do not raise artificial barriers to entry or advancement.

Summary propositions

1 The management of human resources is a vital part of the process of licensed house management.

2 That the key to human resource management is the planning process delineating both the demand and supply of labour for the future.

3 Recruitment and selection are difficult processes to manage and involve key decisions in terms of finding 'round pegs for round holes' – people who fit into the requirements and will wish to stay with the organization.

4 Training and development are key areas in terms of both retention and profitability. A skilled or even multi-skilled workforce is able and willing to contribute to the overall success of the organization.

5 Performance management assists both the manager and the employee. The manager to structure their planning, training and pay systems. The employees to recognize and correct any weaknesses they have and consolidate their future within the industry.

6 Pay is a key area for staff and management alike. Bad management in this area will cause problems not only in terms of turnover, retention or satisfaction but also in the financial prosperity of the company.

Summary questions

1 Why is turnover in the licensed trade industry so high?

2 What methods can we use to reduce turnover?

3 Which are the best media to use in terms recruiting bar staff?

4 What factors affect rates of pay in the industry?

5 Why are tests sometimes unreliable in terms of selection decisions?

6 Why is equality in employment so important?

7 How would you set about training a new member of staff to become a competent bar team member?

Case study

Joseph Sitole has spent 5 years as a manager for a major brewery in a large urban public house. He has now decided to open his own establishment with a view to expanding it into a chain across the UK. Joe has chosen a site close to the centre of Guildford that used to be a furniture store. He has the money to buy it, the concept behind it (the Warehouse), and planning permission. He has started the process of fitting out the premises and has purchased the equipment to go into the unit. He has completed his market research and determined three distinct markets:

1 The student population.

2 Business users from nearby office and a technology park.

3 The local population.

His plans for the units include an upstairs bar (bedrooms and soft furnishings) which will host live music and a host of real ales. A downstairs bar/eatery (carpets) and a 'snug' bar dedicated to alcoholic beverages (upholstery and leather goods). Each area has its own ambience and products. The bedroom will feature discounts and promotional nights, carpets a wide range of both lunchtime and evening meals, and upholstery as a welcoming comfortable refuge from the hurly-burly of life.

The premises are due to open in 6 weeks time and Joseph has just sat back and tried to see if he has missed anything.

'Employees,' he shouted 'what about my staff!' He had put some thought to the matter before but the process of building had driven it from his mind. He sets about in a very methodical way to list what he now has to do.

1 What does Joseph have to put on his list?

2 Which recruitment sources should he use to attract his workforce?

3 What training does he need to do with his staff?

4 How can he make his staff want to stay with him and assist in his planned expansion?

5 What can he do to make his staff his biggest selling point?

References and further reading

Beardwell, I. and Holden, L. (1997). *HRM: A Contemporary Perspective*. Pitman.

DoE (1971). Department of Employment Briefing, Vol. 26.

Graham, H. T. and Bennett, R. (1998). *Human Resource Management*. Pitman.

Lewis, C. (1985). *Employee Selection*. Hutchinson.

Lucas, R. (1995) *Managing Employee Relations in the Hotel and Catering Industry*. Cassell.

Mullins, J. R. (1999). *Management and Organisational Behaviour*. 5th edn. Pitman.

Pigors, P. and Myers, C. S. (1977). *Personnel Administration*. 8th edn. McGraw Hill.

Riley, M. (1996) *HRM In Hospitality and Tourism Industries*. Butterworth-Heineman.

Roberts, J. (2000). *Human Resource Practice in the Hospitality Industry*. Hodder and Stoughton.

Shackleton, V. and Newell, S. (1991). Management selection: a comparative survey of methods. *Journal of Occupational Psychology*. **64**.

Thomson, R. and Mabey, C. (1994). *Developing Human Resources*. Butterworth-Heineman.

Torrington, D. and Hall, L. (1998). *Human Resource Management*. Prentice Hall.

Tyson, S. and York, A. *Human Resource Management*. Elsevier.

CHAPTER 7

Controlling
your profits

Profits are obtained from various sources of income, dependent upon the operation of the establishment. The main source of income in licensed trade premises (50 per cent to 90 per cent) comes from the consumption of beverages, and it is likely that between 50 per cent and 80 per cent of beverage income will derive from beer. Profit on non-alcoholic beverages can also be significant (see Chapter 5). Food is generally the next major income source; how much so depends upon the emphasis placed by the manager or owner. Income gained from gaming machines, and the rental of function rooms are the other two common areas of profit.

Small independent establishments may, with only one or two members of staff plus the licensee, be able to operate using manual control systems, but all large establishments and all chains monitor and control income and expenditure using information technology (IT) systems of varying sophistication. However, even in the smallest of operations the till may be electronic and be able to perform some management functions, or the beer lines may be metered, therefore this chapter concentrates on the IT-based control systems available. It is considered to be good business practice for independent establishments to use external accountants, auditors and stocktakers to assist with the control of profits. Large organizations will have entire departments that specialize in these functions. Further reading about manual systems is suggested at the end of the chapter, and technical details concerning the accounting function can be gleaned from many specialist books.

IT-based systems in the public house

Reliable up-to-date information is key to developing the competitive advantage in the modern public house. Information technology is able to produce accounts quickly and accurately, which can be used as the basis for management decision-making. A manual system will produce similar information, but it is time-consuming and slower.

The major players have invested heavily in sophisticated systems, which they are now totally dependent on for the collection, collation and processing of data affecting all elements of their business, particularly the control of finance. To date the hospitality industry has not utilized IT in food and beverage to its full potential; industries such as retail and banking are using computers as a key resource for competitive and operational analysis, whereas hospitality has focused mainly on reservations and finance.

Technical advances continue to be made and hardware and software need to be constantly updated. The relative infancy of the Internet is going to have a major influence on the future developments, with existing system software and application software being maintained and updated using the Internet. The major players will be able to create their own corporate intranet, to connect organizational networks and information resources together, and to provide common consistent modes of access.

Application software

Sensible use of application software by senior staff can be very effective for management and operational information. The most common applications used in the licensed trade are described in the following sections.

Management information systems

The major players have recognized the importance of management information systems (MIS), which are fast, efficient and able to produce statistical information on all the key areas within the licensed trade and, most importantly, the speed at which the information can be gathered enables management to use the data as a forecasting tool. The planning and preparation of an MIS system is the key to success.

'Firms now have so many diverse opportunities to develop and use information technology that they must rationally plan for those activities' (Raghunthan, in Davis and Lockwood, 1995: 251). The planning must include the systems implementation, which is core to its success. Many systems have failed because management and operators have not used the systems to their

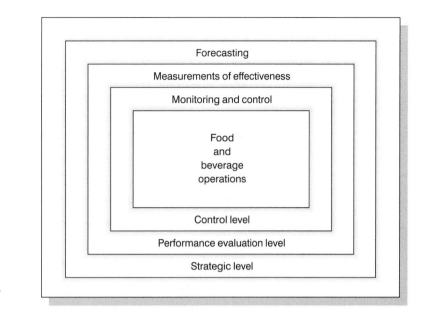

Figure 7.1
Model for MIS function
Source: Davis and Lockwood,
1995: 257.

full potential. Rhodes (in Davis and Lockwood, 1995: 252) identified a number of common themes. These relate to:

- failure to design systems in line with business and operational policies

- failure to rationalize and simplify operational procedures in advance of system implementation

- overeagerness to adopt over-sophisticated systems rather than build systems on basic user needs

- failure to involve all of the users and stakeholders' needs for operational systems development and installation

- failure of management to recognize stakeholders' needs for operational systems rather than centralized bureaucratic systems.

A fully integrated system can be a very effective management tool for measuring projected targets against operational performance. The information gathered can be stored and used for long-term strategic planning.

Catering information systems

The most complex component of an MIS is the control of beverages and food, which in mainstream hospitality can be subcategorized as a catering information system (CIS). Beverage and food control relies on a large database of information from the purchasing and storage of goods, to the delivery of service, to the receipt and control of moneys.

The main benefits of a CIS are the speed the information can be accessed, the accuracy of the data and the ability to control costs. There are numerous systems, which are constantly being updated. The key features (adapted from Davis and Lockwood, 1995: 256) of all the systems are:

1 Control and document all beverage and food-stock items by classification and individual item.

2 Record and cost all store transactions throughout the unit.

3 Calculate values of stores issued, held and demanded, within automatic updating on price changes.

4 Maintain stores levels in all stock locations.

5 Record automatically, at the point of entry or exit from stores, all stock movements by destination, types and costs.

6 Generate purchase orders based on reorder levels.

7 Record purchase orders status, i.e., deliveries awaited, and those partially fulfilled.

8 Update stock levels on receipt of purchase orders.

9 Calculate stock-usage data and generate stock-usage report and wastage reports.

10 Prompt for unit stock checks and generate period-end reports,

and for the recipe/menu planning subsystem:

1 The compilation of menus from an index of recipes.

2 The storage of cycle of menus.

3 The calculation of the specific ingredient requirements based on compiled menu.

4 The generation of a stores requisition to meet the ingredient requirements.

5 The costing of individual menus.

6 The costing of total meal requirements.

7 The ability to plan costed meals for routine and special functions.

8 The analysis of historical data to indicate food usage by type, and to provide a database for developing a demand model.

The initial database can take considerable time to establish, with many pitfalls to overcome. When dealing with food sales, recipes will often use a range of measurements, such as 'a pinch', 'a handful', 'a cup of', 'a dash of', which need to be translated into metric, imperial or liquid measures the computer can understand. Chefs will interpret recipes differently, to add their distinctive flair, therefore it would be difficult for a system to accurately re-order stock based on the recipe costings.

A catering information system is not always considered suitable for small establishments because it is expensive in terms of time and capital to set up and, if food is a significant factor, it can place many constraints on the creativity of the menu as well as the time needed to constantly update.

Stock control systems

Efficient stock control is the key to profitability. Innkeepers need to identify any discrepancies as quickly as possible to rectify the problem. Staff, who are aware of efficient operational controls, are likely to be deterred from any dishonesty.

In its simplest form, any system needs to enter the stock received and issued, to cross-reference against details of consumption and calculate the value of stock in hand. More sophisticated systems will record the details described in the CIS.

Bar stock is considered easier to control than food items. Most managers will be made aware of any deficiencies when the projected gross profits (taking into account the present stock level) is lower than expected. Control of ullage is probably the most complex section, and if not monitored correctly can have a significant effect on profit (see Chapter 5).

Particular consideration must be taken with:

- purchasing and delivery procedures

- ullage

- equipment efficiency (refrigeration, pipe-cleaning, cask control)

- theft

- hospitality (drinks on the house, staff allowance, management allowance).

Food control issues are more complex, leaving management with the dilemma of analysing the root cause. The CIS's key features enable instant access to a significant amount of relevant data. Often the outcome of the research is the identification of one or more of the following:

- theft

- wastage (perishability of products, overpurchasing, expiry of sell-by-dates, portion control)

- costings (fresh food prices fluctuate daily)

- equipment (freezer, fridge breakdown)
- recipe variation (different chefs using different quantities)
- historical data (seasonal changes in profit margins, e.g. Christmas menus tend to be more profitable)
- hospitality (courtesy meals, staff meals, management allowances).

Figure 7.2 illustrates an integrated MIS system, demonstrating that the applications discussed in this chapter can work independently. However, by linking them together, they can interact and become much more efficient and effective by sharing common data to create invaluable management information. The size and the applications required will vary from business to business.

Electronic point of sale

Electronic point of sale (EPOS) systems have taken the place of the traditional cash register. In its simplest form it is a cash register with a processor, memory and printer. The major players

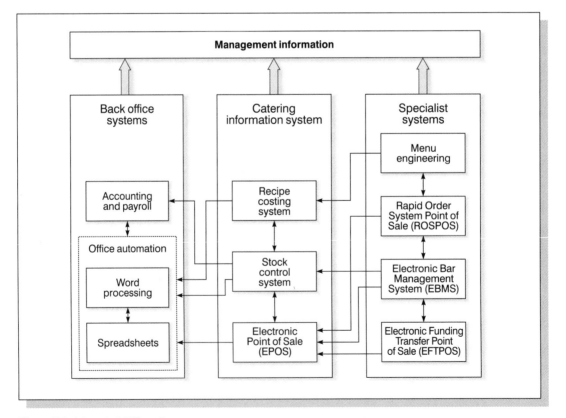

Figure 7.2 Integrated MIS system

have sophisticated systems which are an integral part of the MIS system, offering a range of data that can be used, such as:

- revenue statistics

- sales analysis

- inventory usage

- labour costs

- service productivity

- profitability (McDermid, in Braham, 1993: 43).

Electronic point of sale systems handle transactions at the point of sale. The beverage and food orders are entered, and routed automatically from the point of sale to the point of production, normally also being interfaced into the CIS. As the order is entered, the information is transferred to the bar or kitchen. Most items will be displayed on a touchscreen, which is automatically updated. Non-standard items may be entered manually. Several prices are stored in the event of special offers, 'happy hours', etc. When the customer is ready to pay, an itemized bill is prepared instantly, including the VAT and service charge.

There are several types of EPOS available, counter based or hand held, mainly touchscreen, with useful prompts for staff to avoid mistakes or omissions. For example, if a customer orders a cocktail, the user can note any special requests automatically – for instance, a twist of lemon rather than an olive in a martini. The serving staff are then able to spend more time dealing with the customer's needs, the staff have legible orders which are recorded for analysis of any discrepancies.

Specialized applications

Electronic funds transfer at point of sale

The traditional use of purchasing using cash is undergoing dramatic change. Cashless payment systems are now available in many establishments. Electronic funds transfer at point of sale (EFTPOS) terminals enable customers to open an account for all purchases by swiping a credit card or smart card into the system, creating a direct link to the credit company, enabling fast authorization of the funds available.

Electronic funds transfer at point of sale terminals are able to:

- validate the credit card

- produce the voucher or VAT receipt

- provide instant totals at the end of the shift and day

- remove the administrative burdens of summaries and banking

- remove the problems of clerical errors such as lost vouchers, overlooked expiry dates, etc.

- give a faster, more efficient service to the customer (Braham, 1993: 135).

As previously noted, some establishments are too small to justify the expense, however, larger venues and pub chains are increasingly introducing EFTPOS terminals.

Beverage control systems (electronic bar management system)

The owner of a garage would always account for every last drop of fuel purchased and sold, in order to control revenue, yet the licensed trade does not generally insist on such strict controls, leaving the system open to abuse. A petrol-pump attendant would not be able to offer free petrol to friends, however, many pub employees will openly admit that systems are open to abuse, particularly with spirits and beers which are not preportioned. The installation of an electronic bar management system (EBMS) enables a manager to improve the control and security, with instant revenue records. An EBMS works on the basis of fitting sensors to every optic and beer pump, allowing all the drinks dispensed, either by measure or flow to be accurately measured. Beer monitoring systems can also be fitted to record the number and time of keg changes. The system will calculate the sales, which are then compared with the physical stocktake to identify any discrepancies. The monitoring of the system must be secure and unavailable to unauthorized staff. Specific problems can be pinpointed to individual sales points or individual members of staff in order to investigate any suspicion of fraud.

Rapid order system point of sale

Rapid order system point of sale (ROSPOD) is a hand-held system, no bigger than a calculator, which is capable of communicating with the computer by one of three methods:

- by plugging into a nearby order point

- by radio control

- by infrared technology (Braham, 1993: 48).

The system enables service staff to record an order at the table, ready for transmission to the main computer. A ROSPOD is very useful when the service area is a long distance from the bar or kitchen, perhaps where drinks and food are served in a beer garden or on a terrace.

Menu engineering

'Menu engineering' was a term coined by M. L. Kasvana and D. I. Smith in their book *Menu Engineering: A Practical Guide to Menu Analysis* (published in 1982). This book was an extremely important contribution to pricing through cash gross profit. It's main point, the major breakthrough, is that the percentage approach to pricing and gross profit is seen as simplistic, and it is recognized that:

1 The principle aim of the menu pricing is to secure the right level of cash gross profit.

2 Each menu should make a sufficient contribution to overall profitability in terms of cash gross profit.

Table 7.1 is an example of a menu engineering worksheet, comparing the benefits and constraints of the 10 main courses served on a menu.

The essential aim of menu engineering is to analyse the popularity and profitability of the menu items, and to define each item into one of the four categories identified in Table 7.2. Prior to the introduction of IT within the food and beverage areas, this process was very lengthy and time-consuming, the information not always arriving in time to be useful. Using MIS, once the database has been completed, an analysis of the menu performance can be undertaken at any time, and relevant information obtained immediately. The following list is a manual, column-by-column analysis of the menu engineering sheet shown in Table 7.1.

1 Showing, in respect of each menu item, the total number of items sold during the period under review.

2 The percentage composition of the total of menu items sold.

3 The food cost per portion would be obtained from the establishment's standard recipes, costing sheets, etc. (and the whole package can be linked in one integrated spreadsheet), column 3.

4 The item selling price is the menu price less the VAT element.

5 The cash gross profit per menu item. This is obtained by deducting the cost per portion in column 3 from the selling price in column 4.

6 The total food cost of each menu item is shown. Each figure in this column is obtained by multiplying the relevant number of items sold by the cost per portion shown in column 3.

Menu item	1 No. of items	2 Menu mix %	3 Item food cost	4 Item SP	5 Item CGP	6 Total food cost	7 Total sales	8 Total CGP Amount	%	Rank	9 CGP category	10 MM category	Notes
Sole Veronique	560	14.0	2.85	8.50	5.65	1 596.00	4 760.00	3 164.00	16.5	2	H	H	Star
Grilled trout	500	12.5	2.65	7.95	5.30	1 325.00	3 975.00	2 650.00	13.9	3	H	H	Star
Chicken Kiev	630	15.7	2.55	5.95	3.40	1 606.50	3 748.50	2 142.00	11.2	5	L	H	Plough horse
Roast duck	180	4.5	2.35	7.25	4.90	423.00	1 305.00	882.00	4.6	7	H	L	Puzzle
Calves' liver	210	5.2	2.10	4.75	2.65	441.00	997.00	556.50	2.9	9	L	L	Dog
Leg of lamb	540	13.5	1.95	6.50	4.55	1 053.00	3 510.00	2 457.00	12.9	4	L	H	Plough horse
Lamb chops	190	4.8	1.85	6.25	4.40	351.50	1 187.50	836.00	4.4	8	L	L	Dog
Irish stew	240	6.0	1.95	4.25	2.30	468.00	1 020.00	552.00	2.9	10	L	L	Dog
Sirloin steak	280	7.0	3.10	8.95	5.85	868.00	2 506.00	1 638.00	8.8	6	H	H	Star
Entrecote steak	670	16.8	3.15	9.45	6.30	2 110.50	6 331.50	4 221.00	22.1	1	H	H	Star
	4 000	100				£10 242.50	£29 341.00	£19 098.50	100				

Source: Kotas and Jarawardena, 1994: 254.

Table 7.1 Menu engineering worksheet

7 Total sales in column 7 is obtained by multiplying each number of menu items sold by the appropriate item selling price shown in column 4.

8 Under the heading 'Total CGP' three figures for each menu item are entered. The amount of cash gross profits is, in each case, the difference between the relevant figures in columns 7 and 6. Such figures may also be obtained by multiplying the appropriate amounts in columns 1 and 5. In the next column is showing the percentage composition of cash to profit. Finally in the third column, is shown the ranking of the menu items in terms of the contribution they make to the total cash gross profit.

9 In column 9, all the menu items are categorized in terms of their cash gross profits. This is done by reference to the weighted average cash gross profit. In this case the average cash gross profit per menu item is £4.77 (£19 098.50 ÷ 4000). Menu items with a cash gross profit loading of £4.77 or more are classified as high cash gross profit items (H), whilst those with less than £4.77 are classified as low cash gross profit earners (L).

10 The function of column 10 is to classify the popularity of menu items. With a menu consisting of 10 items one would expect, other things being equal, each item to account for approximately 10 per cent of the menu mix. Any item reaching at least 10 per cent of items sold would be classified as enjoying high popularity (H), and conversely those, which failed to reach the magic 10 per cent, would be classed as having a low popularity (L). Following this approach half the menu items would tend to be shown as below average in terms of popularity. This in turn may call for rather frequent and fundamental revisions of the menu. It is for this reason that the American food service operators who devised this approach to menu analysis use the 70 per cent formula. They would regard all menu items that reach at least 70 per cent of their 'rightful share' of the menu mix as enjoying high popularity. With this approach where a menu consists of 20 items any item which reached 3.5 per cent (70 per cent of 5 per cent) of the menu mix would be regarded as having a high popularity. While there is no convincing theoretical support for choosing 70 per cent rather than another percentage, common sense suggests that there is much merit in this approach.

Remedial action

Having studied or created a menu engineering worksheet, the next step to take is remedial action, especially with regard to those menu items which fall into the 'dog' category on the worksheet.

Stars	These are menu items, which make a significant contribution to menu profitability.
	These items deserve a lot of attention. Nothing must be done to prejudice their success.
	Their quality must be maintained through the purchase of the best possible ingredients, competent food preparation and attractive presentation.
Plough horses	These items do not generate a lot of cash gross profit per item sold but they contribute frequently, being very popular, an overall reasonable amount of profit.
	Whilst it may be tempting to increase plough horse prices and try to convert them to stars, there may well be a significant minority of customers who favour these items because of their price.
	Adjustments to portion *costs* may be possible in certain circumstances.
Puzzles	Here a variety of corrective action is possible. In some cases a lower price may increase their popularity.
	Some of these menu items do not sell well because they do not appear attractive on the menu; a possible solution would be to rename the menu item.
	As a general principle, the longer the shelf life, the stronger the case for retaining the menu item.
Dogs	As a general principle, a dog should be removed, and replaced by a more successful food item.
	While their removal should not necessarily be automatic, it must be remembered that there is a dual problem with the item, it is both low in profit and unpopular.

Source: Kotas and Jarawardena, 1994: 256.

Table 7.2 Remedial action

Gaming machines

Although not strictly part of an integrated IT system, gaming machines can add significantly to the profitability of an establishment, and profits must be controlled along with all other sources of income. The only gaming machines allowed on to conventional licensed house premises, as opposed to private clubs or casinos, are fruit machines and amusement with prizes (AWP) machines. Two fruit machines are the maximum allowed per establishment, and if operated correctly should raise up to 10 per cent of the profit of the establishment, one machine generating about £3000–£4000 per annum. AWP machines, and music machines, do not generate a significant amount of income, so are installed primarily to provide a service to the consumer. The maximum payout permitted on the fruit machines is £10, which is about 85 per cent of the money gambled. To encourage usage of the machines they should be sited close to the bar, so that as the customer turns away from the bar, change in hand, they are tempted to play. Interest in playing is also generated when the machines are new; play being highest in the first couple of months, so machines should be changed approximately every 6 months.

For control and security each machine should contain a 'black box' which records, among other details, what cash went through the machine and at what time it was turned on/off. Sometimes managers forget to turn the machines on and revenue is lost. It is important that a record of how much went through the machine is kept because, for security reasons, they are emptied frequently, but the cash itself is banked by the rental company, not the licensee.

Summary propositions

1 Control of cash and stock is vital to the profitability of an organization.

2 IT and MIS systems can significantly improve management access to information and control of the business, but only if the establishment is large enough to support the initial capital outlay.

3 An MIS system is only useful if it provides management with information that they need.

Summary questions or activities

1 Research details of six software packages suitable for licensed trade premises, listing out the advantages and disadvantages of each package for a chain of café bars.

2 The installation of any MIS system is a major capital investment. Using the packages described in question 1 estimate how long it would take the café bar to gain a suitable return on their investment.

3 Below what level of turnover would it be sensible for the management to retain a simple EPOS control system rather than installing a EFTPOS system?

Case study

A chain of six pubs based in the Alderly Edge area, is considering installing a CIS system, to enable them to monitor their units individually and holistically, prior to the proposed acquisition of two new destination venues. At present the company has an annual turnover of approximately £4 million. It is anticipated that this will rise to £5.5 million with the acquisition of the two new properties.

1 Prepare a feasibility study for the management of the chain, to enable them to make an informed choice about a suitable system for them to install.

2 Plan a strategy for the implementation of the system chosen.

References and further reading

Braham, B. (1993). *Computer Systems in the Hotel and Catering Industry.* Cassell.

Davis, B. and Lockwood, A. (1995). *Food and Beverage Management: A Selection of Readings.* Butterworth-Heinemann.

Dyson, J. R. (1997). *Accounting for Non-Accounting Students.* Pitman.

Kasvana, M. L. and Smith, D. I. (1982). *Menu Engineering: A Practical Guide to Menu Analysis.* Hospitality Publications.

Kotas, R. and Jarawardena, C. (1994). *Profitable Food and Beverage Management.* Hodder and Stoughton.

O'Connor, P. (1996). *Using Computers in Hospitality.* Cassell.

Owen, G. (1994). *Accounting for Hospitality, Tourism and Leisure.* Pitman.

Pappas, M. J. (1997). *Eat Foods Not Profits! How Computers can Save your Restaurant.* Van Nostrand Reinhold.

Wood, F. (1977). *Business Accounting 1.* Pitman.

Ethics and dilemmas: the challenges of the licensed trade industry

Conservative administrations, have, for the past 18 years, pursued a policy of deregulation in respect of alcohol sales and self-regulation in respect of policing the industry. This has been wholly consistent with its wider ideological perspectives on a free market only minimally constrained by bureaucratic or political interference. Thus we have seen major relaxations in licensing laws, the deregulation of Sunday drinking and the encouragement of family visits to pubs. These changes have been largely welcomed by the public, the drinks industry and in particular those parties keen to harmonise with European social habits and create 24-hour cities.

The drinks industry has throughout this period, quite simply, got on with its primary mission: making a profit from producing and selling [alcoholic] drinks (and food). . . . This is a respectable business ethic (Brain and Parker, 1999).

Herein lies the dilemma for the alcoholic beverages industry. How to follow their legitimate, and generally popular, business mission of making a profit from alcoholic beverages while also ensuring that the environments in which these sales take place is safe, attractive to the moderate majority, unappealing to the delinquent minority and in compliance with legal dictates.

As the licensed trade industry has become more deregularized, various groups have been set up or have evolved to assist in the maintenance of safe environments in which the majority of moderate consumers can relax, socialize and consume alcoholic or non-alcoholic beverages as part of their overall leisure activities. Some of the most important groups are the Portman Group, Alcohol in Moderation and the British Institute of Innkeepers. See Chapter 9 for further details about these and other related groups.

The purpose of this chapter is:

- to raise awareness of the ethical and moral dilemmas which constantly face a responsible licensed house manager or owner

- to highlight instances of good practice

- to indicate where further information can be sought, which will be up to date, when the prospective licensed house manager or owner applies for their justices licence.

It is not possible to give definitive answers to the points raised in this chapter because

- the types of beverages available

- how they are marketed and perceived

- the increasing amount and changing use of leisure time

- the general increase in disposable income

mean that the environment within which beverages and food are sold is constantly changing. It is intended that this chapter will be thought-provoking and a useful basis for discussion rather than prescriptive.

The management of violence

Alcohol acts as a mood changer, in the same way as do other more commonly recognized drugs such as cannabis, cocaine or ecstasy. For most people alcohol in moderation will cause them to become more relaxed and sociable, however, some people have an instant reaction to alcohol, and while some people who have drunk too much go to sleep, and others become giggly, a significant number of people, both men and women, become aggressive. This is a major cause of violence on licensed premises. Another cause of aggression can be simple frustration – when a customer comes in to relax and cannot get to the bar, finds their favourite drink is not available, gets jostled and drink is spilt, or any combination of these three. There may also be occasions, which fortunately are not common, when people enter the premises just to look for or make trouble, just to extend the 'high' that they are already on.

These are the main reasons why violence occurs, and there are several actions which the manager, and their staff can and should take to ensure that the potential for trouble is reduced as far as possible. Reducing violence will obviously reduce the risk of damage to property and people, and trade generally benefits when customers perceive a licensed premises as a safe and secure environment in which to relax. Not all establishments are high risk, country pubs are likely to have much less trouble than town centre establishments, and not all days are the same – Friday and Saturday nights tend to have the highest number of violent or other antisocial incidents occurring. If violence is persistently allowed to occur on licensed premises the police have the right to have the liquor licence revoked, and the business closed down (see Chapter 3 for further details). In an efficient and well-run pub the aggressive frustration caused by bad service should not occur. Staff should be trained so that on those odd occasions when a popular beverage is not available they are able to offer suitable alternatives. Staff who do not know what they are serving merely increase customer frustration. Many of the best methods of reducing violence include training, and several positive areas of activity are discussed here.

Management and staff training schemes

A study carried out by Nottingham University in 1994 found that only 6 per cent of licensees said that they had never had an incident in their pub (where incidents included verbal abuse, such as the aggressive drunk at closing time). Other more recent studies have shown similar findings. As a result it is now common for all companies owning or running licensed premises to run courses aimed at showing staff, including door staff, how to recognize, diffuse and then manage potentially difficult situations. Much of the training includes information on how to remain calm, how to use body language and speech, but also how to recognize when nothing can stop the situation blowing and so to call in external help, i.e., the police. Some large companies publish in-house training manuals for their trainers, such as Allied Domecqs' *Keeping Pubs Peaceful*. For smaller companies or independent licensees there are professional bodies that provide courses, either in house or at various educational establishments, courses such as NVQs/SVQs, or those provided by the BII as part of their whole professional portfolio. For more details on courses available see Chapter 9.

Doorstaff

Doorstaff, security staff, stewards, all formerly known collo-quially as 'bouncers', have been used for a long time on licensed premises to monitor people who want to enter the establish-ments. Originally they were employed primarily by those establishments which had a public entertainment licence (PEL, see Chapter 3) to ensure that those people who were allowed in were not drunk, carrying drugs or likely to cause trouble in any other way. Now they are likely to be employed by a variety of venues, and the employment of registered doorstaff may be a condition of the justices licence. The idea was that violence on the premises could be reduced if unsuitable persons were not allowed in in the first place. However, 'bouncers' came to have a very unfortunate reputation; past police records show that many incidents of violence were caused by the 'bouncers' themselves and they were sometimes part of the drug-dealing organizations. Doorstaff now do not, in general, belong to this genre.

The purpose of doorstaff is to monitor those who enter the premises, tactfully refuse those whom it would not be suitable to let in, perhaps because they are already drunk or, perhaps, merely because the establishment is full and some current customers will have to leave before others can be allowed in. In some establishments they may also be required to search customers entering the premises for weapons and drugs. They also monitor the situation internally and should be on hand, like the licensee in a smaller venue, to tactfully diffuse a situation as it starts to happen and long before it has become dangerous. To do all this, doorstaff need to be trained professionally and in most areas there is a local registration scheme which the doorstaff need to belong to before they can be employed. It is the responsibility of the licensee to ensure that their doorstaff are properly qualified. This can be quite difficult if the licensee subcontracts their doorstaff from a local security firm, as many do. The licensee should check, that the security firm trains its staff properly before any contract is signed. One of the problems with local schemes is that, although they may all check the criminal record of applicants, the standard of training can be very variable and so, if doorstaff move around the UK, they may be required to retrain in the next area they move to. As registration can cost from £15 to £200 a time, this can be a great disincentive. As a result of this the government sponsored an initiative to set up a national scheme. The Door Staff scheme became available at the end of 1998, and the qualification is awarded jointly by the BII and the Security Industry Training Organization (SITO). Some

NVQs and SVQs have also been developed. It is likely that these national qualifications will take over from the local registration schemes.

Design of the premises

Even with good training and an effective staff and management team, some premises are difficult to work in – a listed building, for instance, built several centuries ago when ceilings were lower, and over time extended with the addition of new rooms often on slightly different levels. While this may be considered by tourists and some customers to be quaint and cosy, these establishments can be a nightmare for staff. Not only can they make efficient service difficult, they can also encourage antisocial behaviour when seating, toilet entrances and so on are out of sight of the bar staff. Most incidents of violence and other antisocial behaviour start in blind spots; this would include, among others, drug dealing and the sale of stolen goods. This is a major problem for licensees, they need to be able to see all areas from the bar, but an open-plan style may not seem welcoming to some groups of customers who want to feel, psychologically at least, private. If there is trouble in an open-plan establishment, the aggression can quickly flow from the initial problem group and infect the whole establishment. Smaller rooms are better for the containment of aggressive behaviour.

Sometimes it is quite simple for the licensee to remove internal partition walls, opening up the blind spots and yet retaining the psychological feeling of group intimacy by the use of low-backed banquet seating, booth seating, trellised dividers, etc. In other establishments, or when it comes to the changing of toilet entrances and fire exit doors, this may be significantly harder. Reports by the Portman Group show that almost half of the incidences of disorder take place within or near to the toilets. Fire doors that are not visible need to be alarmed to discourage unwelcome behaviour by delinquent customers opening the door to let in younger friends for instance.

Apart from the need to consult the local fire authorities, local planning authorities, and inform the local magistrates of all major structural changes to licensed premises, it may not be physically possible to open up all of the blind spots. Traditionally this problem has been overcome by the judicious positioning of mirrors, so that from the bar all customer areas can be seen, however, these can seem a little indiscreet. A closed circuit television (CCTV) camera, with the monitor behind the bar can be more discreet, and more useful in the aftermath of an incident. The obvious positioning of CCTV cameras can be useful if the idea of the observation is to deter criminal behaviour, although it may put off some consumer groups. Licensees need to find a balance for their particular establishment.

It should be remembered that as one of the causes of aggression is jostling and spillages, as people pass to and from the bar with drinks, simply opening up the access routes to and from the bar by moving, slightly reducing or repositioning the (movable) seats and tables may quickly reduce aggression levels without any cost being involved. The use of some fixed seating should be considered as it will both reduce the amount of furniture that can be used in a fight (note how heavy the furniture often is), and there will be less furniture for the customers to move around themselves, and so less likelihood of the bar access routes being blocked accidentally. If furniture is moved around, once the group has left, bar staff should replace the furniture in its original position to facilitate customer flow.

In many new establishments, or where a major refurbishment is being undertaken the bar may be raised above the general floor level. This both helps the bar staff to retain good sight lines over the whole area, especially potential trouble spots such as the pool table and fruit machines, and also often enables them to see, and establish the service order, of customers waiting to be served. Frustration builds if a customer feels that they are being overlooked by bar staff when it is their 'turn' to be served.

In high-risk premises, good bar design would also incorporate a 'safe room' accessed from behind the bar, and containing a telephone connected directly to the local police station.

Pool tables and amusement machines

Some police forces will encourage the licensee to remove pool tables from pubs, others may restrict the number of tables permitted, yet others may insist on close and obvious CCTV monitoring. The reason for this is because the pool table and its equipment can be a significant trigger for violent aggression, both the cues and the balls making very dangerous weapons. Arguments generally arise when there is no clear set of rules as to house custom for how games are 'booked', and non-locals act in a way which may be acceptable in their local but not in the present one. Another flash-point tends to be jostling; this time not just drinks spillage, but also knocking the cue during play. Potential for violence can be reduced if the cues and spare balls are kept behind the bar and have to be requested and returned; if the house playing rules are clearly stated next to each pool table; if the practice of laying money down on the table to 'book' the next game is discouraged and if there is sufficient space around each table. The pool table area should be regularly monitored both by distant observation, and staff patrols, glass collecting, ashtray emptying or whatever.

Fruit (and music) machines can also be potential trouble spots. Frustration can be caused by many incidents – a run of bad luck, jostling at a critical moment, noise levels or type of music. As all these machines need to be fed money to work they are also targets of theft, or unsuccessful theft which equates to vandalism. As with pool tables these machines need to be kept under constant observation, they also need to be placed well away from the entrance, so as to reduce the likelihood of opportunistic theft.

In some establishments significant amounts of extra revenue are generated by pool tables and entertainment machines (see Chapter 7), both in terms of beverages consumed during play and the cost of each new play. Where the games are not significant revenue earners licensees should consider whether or not the potential to trigger aggression outweighs the income generated.

Glasses

Drinking straight from the bottle has a large following amongst certain groups of consumers, especially the 18 to 24 age group, and for certain drinks, e.g. RTDs and premium beers, as previously discussed, but the vast majority of beverages are sold in glasses, including all bulk dispensed beverages. However, glass either as a bottle or as a drinking glass has the potential to be used as a lethal disfiguring weapon. Glass can also cause significant damage in much more innocuous situations, for instance, a flamboyant hand movement can clear a table of glasses, some may smash and the flying shards quite easily cut a person or, if outdoors, be left in the grass for a toddler to fall on.

For these reasons much work is currently being done on the production of toughened glasses. These glasses are designed to crumble into small fairly harmless crystals, in the same way as a car windscreen is designed to honeycomb rather than shatter when broken, thus rendering the glass unsatisfactory as a weapon, hard to break and useless when broken. In high-risk venues, some local authorities will not issue a public entertainment licence (see Chapter 3) unless toughened glass is used, and will ban the sale of drinks in glass bottles. In response to this, and in response to consumer demand to drink from the bottle, some companies, such as Bass, Carlsberg-Tetley and Brains now sell many of those beverages that are commonly drunk from the bottle in specially designed plastic (PET) bottles, again reducing their usefulness as a weapon, and making it unlikely that they could cause hurt to anyone.

Most consumers are peaceful and law abiding, and most licensees would not want to change their range of glasses to the currently quite restricted range of toughened glasses available. However, as the example given earlier illustrates, glasses are fragile and can cause serious accidents. Therefore it is sensible in all establishments for the management to ensure that empty glasses are collected frequently. If glasses are left to pile up on the tables, they look untidy and, as new customers stack them up haphazardly to create space, they become a danger. Each broken glass represents lost profit. Profits are also lost if the bar staff cannot serve new customers because there are no clean glasses behind the bar. The customer, delayed while waiting for glasses to be washed, is likely to become irritated both by the delay and again when their beer is finally served, by inexperienced staff, in a hot glass freshly taken from the glass-washer. This kind of fault causes damage, both to the immediate atmosphere in the venue and to its long-term image.

Collecting glasses can also serve another function; if a licensee wants to check out a certain part of the premises, he or she can legitimately go to that area to collect empties. If the situation looks potentially difficult a friendly, appropriate, word often defuses the tension and the incident passes without developing any further. In other circumstances, when a member of the bar staff is collecting glasses they can report similar potential incidents to the licensee or security staff and, again, trouble can be prevented before it begins. Cleaning ashtrays at the table serves the same hygiene, safety and monitoring processes.

Pubwatch or clubwatch schemes

As part of the overall process of reducing aggression and creating a safe, relaxed environment, most licensees belong to a pubwatch scheme; in fact joining may be a requirement of the licence in England and Wales. As defined by the Portman Group, a

> watch is necessarily a locally driven initiative set up to tackle problems of crime and disorder within the context of a particular community. A watch is essentially a communications network between licensees and police, which provides all parties with an early warning system to prevent escalation and spread of trouble. The success of a watch depends on the commitment of all the watch members and collaboration between police and licensees. Where it is well publicised, pubwatch can act as a powerful deterrent against crime and disorder and help to create a safer drinking environment (St John-Brooks, 1998).

Generally the same type of establishment bands together, i.e., it is a pubwatch, shopwatch, clubwatch, etc. However, in those areas where there are only a few licensed premises, they may all work together as a single group.

The group usually consists of around fifteen establishments, and when trouble occurs the police are telephoned, and so is the next contact on the watch. This means that within a few minutes of trouble occurring local establishments are informed and, if a troublemaker (or group of troublemakers) is ejected, they will find their way into the next establishment barred. If they cannot get in they cannot make trouble on licensees' premises; if they cause a disturbance in the street they are likely to be arrested. Good doorstaff can be a valuable part of the watch, both in preventing undesirable people from entering the establishment, and by alerting other establishments if an incident happens outside their establishments, and the protagonists move on.

This same type of system works with persistent troublemakers whom the group may choose to exclude from their establishments either via a legal Exclusion Order (see Chapter 3) or unofficially as an agreement within the group. Where there are very few licensed premises, the threat of being excluded by all the venues on the watch is often enough, if believed, to stop the persistent troublemaker. Smaller watches usually communicate via the telephone. In high-density urban areas there may be a very large watch, in which case they usually communicate via a paging system. The local police normally have officers dedicated to working with licensees, and further information about pubwatch or clubwatch schemes can be gained either from them, and/or local licensees.

Prevention of under-age drinking

Serving drinks to under-age drinkers is a serious offence, and one for which licensees may well have their licence removed permanently, if the offence is committed persistently. The onus is on licensees and their staff to ensue that all due diligence has been shown if someone underage has been served and a prosecution is bought. It is the responsibility of licensees to ensure that their staff do not knowingly serve under-age drinkers, therefore most companies have in-house training schemes which both make staff members aware of the legal situation and teach good practice when trying to establish someone's age. This is an area where good social skills are important; a person celebrating their eighteenth birthday looks no older than they did the day before, but the likelihood is that some of the party may still be under age. Some people of 21 can look under age, and some 16 year olds look 21; it depends upon the physical and mental maturity of each individual. Good practice calls for the situation to be kept neutral and impersonal, and the best system is for the establishment to have a well-publicized identification requirement policy. An obvious notice that says it is establishment policy to ask for proof of age if people look under age can reduce the personal element of a request for proof of age quite successfully.

However, this then raises the question of what is a suitable form of identity. In 1997/8 in a Cardiff student union bar, student union cards, with pictures, were taken as proof of age, as they were in most of the other licensed premises within the city, until it was pointed out that for historical reasons the university also had some further education (FE) courses, whose students were 16 to 17 years old. These FE students were entitled to student union cards, as members of the university, and had been making full use of them.

In 1990 'Prove It' scheme was launched by the Portman Group to try to solve this dilemma. Licensees, both on- and off-trade, were issued with a form that someone who had been refused service because they appeared to be under age could fill in and send off to the Portman Group, making the refusal less personal, and confirming that, with proof, they would be served in future. The Portman Group would then verify the information and issue a 'Prove It' card to the applicant. There are very few fraudulent applications. The cards are the same size as credit cards and easily carried. Initially the scheme was free, but ever increasing numbers forced the Portman Group, in 1997, to start charging. Although the scheme is still free to applicants, a 'Prove It' kit for licensees (50 application forms) costs £58 + VAT. However, if the establishment is part of the scheme, i.e., has notices displayed to that effect near the entrance, etc., and can show that they actively ask for proof of age and recommend that people refused apply for Prove It cards, then should an incident arise the licensee will be viewed much more sympathetically than one who is not able to prove that they try to deter underage drinking. Research by the Portman Group and others shows that where there is an active policy of asking for proof of age very little underage drinking occurs.

Other common and accepted proofs of identity (ID) are passports, although they are very bulky to carry, especially to a nightclub, and the new drivers' licences which have photographs on them. Only ID that incorporates the owner's photograph should be accepted.

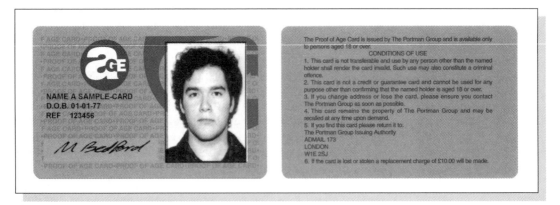

Figure 8.1 Specimen Portman Group proof of age card

Drinking (and driving)

> The scientific data are quite clear: moderate alcohol consumption, especially wine, should be considered a part of a healthy lifestyle. We, as professors, will do what we can to make sure that the public, the medical community and policy-makers are kept up to date on the scientific findings. These findings are now very clear, and to support what St Thomas Aquinas said over 700 years ago: 'if a man abstains from wine to such an extent that he does serious harm to his nature, he will not be free from blame!' (Ellison, 1999: 29–30)

The scientific community is now coming to the belief that alcohol in moderation can be good for people, it can help to lower cholesterol, it may contain antioxidants which can reduce the risks of blood clotting and it can help to lower the risk of heart disease. However, the key word is 'moderation'. The current government recommendations are 21 units per week for women and 28 units per week for men. This should be spread out over the whole week so that binge drinking is avoided. A unit equals 8 g of alcohol or 10 ml of alcohol by volume. The current legal limit for drinking is measured by the blood alcohol concentration (BAC). This is currently set at 80 mg of alcohol in 100 ml of blood, or 35 micrograms in 100 ml of breath (the breathalyser test). This level may be reached by the consumption of two or three units, and each unit takes 1 hour to be processed by the human body. In order for the licensee to keep an orderly house they need to know how many units are contained in different drinks, as do consumers, hence the need to display ABV levels on price lists. It is not always easy for people to work out how many units they have consumed. See Table 8.1, which shows how complex it can be to be absolutely sure of the level of consumption.

As the report *Which Way Forward* (Clayton, 1997) shows, although the government has considered reducing the drink-driving level to 50 mg/100ml BAC, studies throughout the world show that the UK has one of the best records for drink-driving accidents, even though the current BAC level is higher than other countries such as Canada, Sweden and Finland. It would appear that there are several reasons for this. Two to three units consumed during 1 evening, means that a pint of normal beer, a couple of whiskies, etc., can be consumed without the need to worry excessively about being over the limit, so the majority of people stick to the limit because it is achievable. In countries with lower limits, which are not realistically achievable, less people stick to the limit and there is less social stigma attached to being found over the limit. A BAC level of 50 mg/100 ml would mean just over one unit, half a pint, and not even one bottle of many

(a) Beer, lager and cider

Approx strengths (% of alcohol by volume)	Small can ($\frac{1}{2}$ pint/2440 ml)	Standard can (440 ml)	Large can (1 pint/568 ml)	Flagon (1 litre)
Low alcohol: <1.2%; Mild: 2.5%		Whitbread Mild 1 unit	Tennant's LA 1 unit	
Ordinary: 3.%	Foster's lager 1 unit	Whitbread Pale 1.5 units	Carlsberg Lager 2 units	
Export/Strong: 5.0%	Foster's lager (375 ml) 2 units	Newquay Premium 2.5 units	Tennant's Extra (500 ml) 2.5 units	
		Strongbow Cider 2.5 units	Scrumpy Jack Cider 3 units	Strongbow Cider 5.5 units
Special/Super: 9%	Diamond White Cider 2 units	Carlsberg Special Brew 4 units	Tennant's Super 4.5 units	Merrydown Cider 8 units

(b) Wines and spirits

Approx strengths (% of alcohol by volume)	Standard measure	Home measure	Bottle (75 cl)	Litre
Burgundy/Claret 12.5%	125 ml = 1.5 units	2 units	9 units	12 units
Sherry/Port: 18%	60 ml = 1 unit	2 units	13.5 units	18 units
Whisky: 40%	25 ml = 1 unit	2 units	28 units	40 units

Note: 1 unit = 10 ml alcohol by volume = 8 g alcohol.
Source: Stuttaford, 1997.

Table 8.1 Effects of alcohol: units of alcohol per beverage measure

premium beers (as they tend to be stronger that the standard beers). The most effective systems seem to work on a combined basis of an achievable target, strict social pressure and intense periodic publicity campaigns that keep the danger and socially unacceptable nature of drunkenness in the forefront of people's minds.

Modern drinks, premium beers and new world wines all tend to be much higher in alcohol than standard drinks, and licensees (and staff) need to be aware of how much is actually being consumed. As mentioned previously, the size of the glasses used for a glass of wine can significantly alter the consumer's intake without them necessarily being aware of this fact, if the sizes of the glasses are not obviously stated. Likewise with 'doubles' bars, and the actual level of alcohol in various cocktails.

Bearing all this in mind licensees have the responsibility of not allowing consumers on their premises to become drunk or, more realistically, not allowing them to become socially unacceptable or dangerously drunk. If they allow people to become drunk, especially if the customer did not know how much alcohol they had consumed because of large 'house' measures, and an accident occurs, the licensee may be held responsible. This is particularly true in the case of drink-driving where the licensee, or bar staff, knows that someone is drinking heavily and intends to drive home but does nothing about it.

It is recommended that bars develop attractive 'Drivers' shelves' where a range of interesting soft drinks can be displayed. Other measures, which can be taken at the appropriate time, include 'free soft drinks for drivers' promotions, of the kind that many nightclubs used over the millennium New Year's Eve. In this promotion drivers handed over their car keys, received free soft drinks all evening and the rest of the party could drink without worrying. The added advantage to the management of the nightclubs was that many parties had at least one entirely sober person, who could help to diffuse any alcohol-related incidents.

Another initiative is the Portman Group's 'I'll be DES' (designated driver) scheme, launched in October 1999. It is backed by such luminaries as Gary Lineker, Graeme le Saux, Alan Hansen and John Barnes, and although aimed specifically at reducing the drink-driving problem at sporting events, its holistic aim is to appeal to the hard core of young men whom other drink-drive campaigns do not seem to effect.

As with underage drinking, licensees must be seen by the police and other relevant authorities to be taking active steps to prevent drunken behaviour on their premises so that, should any incident arise, they are more likely to be able to put forward their case with an increased chance of success. (See *Munro* vs *Porthkerry Park Holiday Estates Ltd* (1984), in Peters, 1996: 114, for an example.)

Drug misuse

The recreational misuse of drugs is a problem in many sections of society. The effects of drug use can be seriously increased if the drugs are consumed in conjunction with alcohol. Although certain social groups within society suggest that designer drugs are just part of an overall lifestyle, research, police records and mortuary lists would suggest otherwise.

From licensees' point of view the sale or use of drugs on their premises is illegal and condoning the sale or use of them can cause their licence to be revoked, permanently. Vigilance is required to ensure that drug dealing and use does not take place on the premises. Portman Group research suggests that most licensees have most of their trouble within the first 6 months of taking over new premises, when the new management style is bedding down, and local 'entrepreneurs' may take advantage of a new untested face. Typically, dealing of all kinds is occurring when one or two individuals sit quietly and discreetly, preferably in a blind spot, and slowly drink a few drinks, and these individuals are sought by others who probably do not drink at the bar. These others stay a short while, talk and go, perhaps via the toilets or another blind spot. There may also be others in the main part of the bar area who come in with the first individual/s, do not sit with them, but spend their time drinking slowly and watching the day go by 'minding' their own business. All of these actions may be entirely legitimate and coincidental, but they are probably not. Rizla paper, screwed up bits of foil and the filters from unsmoked cigarettes left in ashtrays would suggest drug usage, as would white powder on a tiled ledge in a toilet area.

Preventative measures include not having any blind spots, the licensee and bar staff making the effort to get into conversation with all customers, ensuring that fire exits are alarmed, and that toilet areas cannot be easily used for drug consumption, perhaps by washing the tiled shelves with heavy doses of bleach and, ultimately, changing the smooth tiled window ledge for a rough painted plaster one. The obvious introduction of CCTV cameras also may prove a severe disincentive to criminals.

Permanent recommended measures include contact with the local police, and other licensees in the area via the local watch scheme. This contact helps to identify problem areas quickly and also to develop a good support group, especially when the licensee is still new and finding his or her way in the business and local environment.

Environmental issues

Environmental issues concern areas such as noise pollution, smoking, and litter. Noise pollution from nightclubs is usually not an issue since the clubs have to insulate their premises so as not to disturb the neighbourhood; they also prefer to concentrate the music internally, to produce the required volume for their customers. Music from pubs, noise during the during the day if the establishment has a garden, or drinking on the street if permitted, as well as noise of drunken chatter, cars revving up and doors slamming at closing time are generally the major problems. The majority of the public likes to relax in sociable, affable surroundings. Those who have to live next door to the pub or club may not be so happy. Hence many late night establishments are situated in commercial or specially designated leisure areas, away from residential areas. If venues are in residential areas, licensing authorities may put restrictions on the closing times to reflect the living patterns of people working nearby.

If there is external drinking there is also the problem of litter and broken glass. The broken glass problem has been greatly reduced in recent years by the introduction of toughened glass and PET bottles, but this still leaves the problem of general litter. A condition of the licence might be to employ a member of staff to continuously work in the external areas simply to ensure that there is no litter, as with most fast-food/takeaway establishments. It may be a management decision to ensure that there is no litter, so that good neighbour relationships are established and maintained – some of the neighbours are likely to be customers. Good neighbourliness also extends to traffic congestion from parked cars. If the local residents are unable to park because of the pub's customers, this will lead to a bad relationship. However, if an establishment with ample parking allows people living near by occasionally to use some of their space when they have a large number of visitors this can actively promote a good local neighbour relationship.

Smoking is a much more difficult issue to solve. Traditionally pubs are places where people go to drink, smoke, chat and relax with their friends. If smoking is banned then consumers may as well buy from the off-licence and stay at home. Research would show that a larger proportion of non-smokers will go where smoking is permitted if it means that their groups of friends are all relaxed, than the proportion of smokers who will go to non-smoking environments, because they will not be able to relax. While most people would nowadays consider that it is very bad manners to smoke if others are eating, most people would not consider that smoking and drinking is antisocial. Purchases of cigarettes, although decreasing in some sectors of the population, are on the increase with young females, and cigar purchases have risen phenomenally over the past few years among the higher disposable income groups, therefore, the banning of smoking throughout licensed premises does not seem to make sense. Yet even smokers would prefer not to leave smelling of stale cigarette smoke, and dancing with a lit cigarette is obviously very dangerous for everyone nearby (and so banned in reputable establishments). A survey conducted in 1999 by *The Publican* noted that nearly 50 per cent of customers smoked, and 89 per cent of publicans thought that banning smoking would be bad for their business. Research also shows that inhaling smoke, yours or secondary, can be very bad for the health, and yet in certain circumstances it helps the socializing. Therefore, the licensed trade is in a dilemma at the moment, and always will be in this context.

The government has put the onus firmly on the industry to find a solution to this problem, or they will bring in legislation to ban smoking totally if voluntary self-regulation does not work. As a result various bodies, such as the BII and the Association of Licensed Multiple Retailers (ALMR), have got together to promote AIR (Atmosphere Improves Results). The aim of this charter for self-regulation is to improve the air quality in licensed trade premises, but not necessarily by banning smoking. Separate areas for smokers and non-smokers, especially where the establishment has several rooms, can be set aside, and proper ventilation systems installed which remove not just smoke, but also other personal odours which can be just as unpleasant in confirmed spaces. At the moment professional bodies and employers in the licensed trade industry are working in this area to meet the aims of the charter and improve the quality of air; the government is monitoring the situation.

Recycling is also sometimes mentioned as an issue within licensed trade premises. As previously discussed, if the licensee is not recycling any containers then they are losing a great deal of money which will significantly affect the profitability of the business. Beyond this there are councils that have good recycling schemes which only involve the staff and management in packaging the waste correctly. It is then collected up as part of the general refuse collection system. Any additional costs are usually nominal.

Summary propositions

1 In order to develop new customer bases the licensed trade needs to take advantage of new products and new marketing ploys. This must be balanced against the harm that can be done to vulnerable groups in society.

2 A badly run pub or nightclub is a dangerous environment that will attract the delinquent minority, and may eventually cause the licensee to lose his or her licence.

3 A well-run pubwatch or clubwatch scheme can help all on-trade premises in an area by passing of information; the discussion, and so reduction, of problems and ensuring close accurate liaison with the local police.

Summary questions

1 You think that your establishment may have started to be used for the sale of stolen goods. What action should you take?

2 What qualifications are required by doorstaff in your area?

3 What is a pubwatch or clubwatch scheme?

4 What are the advantages and disadvantages of changing to toughened glass?

Case study

The Moonshade Pub in Newcastle was taken over by new management 3 months ago. The management has recently become aware that the pub is starting to be used for the sale of drugs, particularly cocaine.

1 How is the management likely to have become aware of the problem?

2 What is likely to happen to the business if they take no action?

3 What actions *should* they, and what actions *must* they take to stop the premises being used for this purpose?

References and further reading

Brain, K. and Parker, H (1999). *Drinking with Design, Alcopops, Designer Drinks and Youth Culture*. First published 1997. Portman Group.

Clayton, A. (1997). *Which Way Forward: A Review of Drink Driving Countermeasures in Selected Countries World-Wide*. Portman Group

Ellison, C. (1999). Alcohol and health: an update. *Harpers Wine and Spirit Weekly*, **5931**, 29–30.

Nottingham University (1994). *Working in Public Houses: A Study of the Licensee's Job in Keeping the Peace*. Portman Group.

Peters, R. (1996). *Essential Law for Catering Students*. 2nd edn. Hodder and Stoughton.

St John-Brooks, K. (1998). *Keeping the Peace: A Guide to the Prevention of Alcohol-Related Disorder*. Portman Group.

Stuttaford, T. (1997). *To Your Good Health! The Wise Drinkers Guide*. Faber and Faber.

Walker, A. (1997). *Prove It! Proof of Age Card Scheme*. Portman Group.

Careers and contacts

Many people successfully carving out a career for themselves in the licensed trade started out behind a bar to earn extra money while training for their 'proper job' or in a gap year. They were bitten by the licensed trade bug and never left the industry. It is also true to say that until the late 1990s there were very few courses dedicated to the licensed trade so that an enthusiast could study to enter the licensed trade as a 'proper' job. This is now changing due to the expansion of the industry, increased awareness of the contribution that beverages, etc., make to the overall profits of many businesses and because leisure time and disposable income, both of which are dissipated within licensed trade premises, are on the increase. There are specialist courses from NVQ and SVQ up to degree level, and technical qualifications are looked for by the issuing authorities before a liquor licence will be granted.

Figure 9.1 shows a natural career progression route within the licensed trade industry.

Vocational and professional qualifications

Licensed (Retail) Trade falls within the generic Hospitality Industry and there are certain recognized lead bodies for the hospitality industry. Obtaining their vocational and/or professional qualifications will improve career prospects, e.g., Business and Technician Education Council (BTEC) and NVQ/SVQ (see the list of abbreviations at the end of this chapter for all abbreviations used in this chapter). If in any

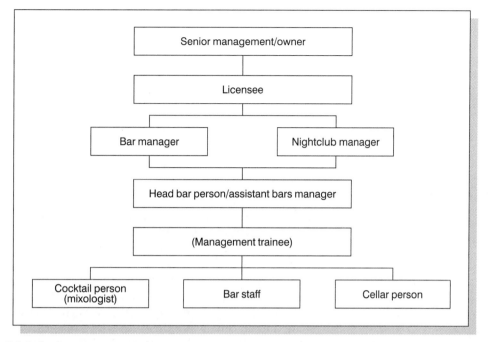

Figure 9.1 Indicative career progression pattern

doubt about qualifications and training, write to one of the professional bodies or trade associations, or to a prospective employer to clarify the recognition and status of the particular qualification you are considering. Before enrolling on a course, make sure that it will lead to relevant, recognized/accredited qualifications. There are some private training companies whose courses are not accredited nationally or internationally and so are not recognized by most employers.

There are currently three 'core' sets of qualifications, one of which will be suitable for the level at which entry to the industry is proposed. In addition to these core courses, other shorter qualifications can be taken which will add value to the overall educational profile. Described below are the three 'core' sets of qualifications, and those shorter qualifications that are most valued by employers, magistrates, bank managers and other relevant authorities

It should be noted that the 'core' qualifications may be divided into lower and more advanced qualifications, further education and higher education. The government has accredited each qualification with a level, 1 to 5, and accreditation at a lower level allows for progression to a higher-level qualification. For instance an NVQ/SVQ level 3, GNVQ Advanced and two A levels, are all accredited at the same level, 3, and so all can lead to level 4 qualifications, i.e., an HND, or possibly a degree if the grade awarded for the level 3 qualification is high enough.

The three 'cores' are:

- NVQ/SVQ qualifications
- BTEC qualifications
- degree and postgraduate qualifications.

Each core and the lead bodies who administer each qualification will be discussed.

NVQ/SVQ

The government set up the National Council for Vocational Qualifications (NCVQ) in 1986. Its aim was to standardize vocational qualifications (NVQ/SVQ) throughout the UK and enable students to acquire competencies at a speed that suited the individual. The NCVQ aims to ensure that its qualifications are based upon the requirements of industry and commerce. They are all vocational and primarily work based, but some NVQ/SVQs are taught on a full-time basis at colleges of further education, TECs, LECs and T&EAs. the NCVQ accredits the wide range of NVQ/SVQs available at four levels:

- Level 1: operative level, simple tasks
- Level 2: operative level, more complex tasks, with some responsibility
- Level 3: supervisory level
- Level 4: management.

An SVQ is the Scottish equivalent of the English and Welsh NVQ. All NVQ/SVQ qualifications consist of mandatory units – units which must be gained for full completion of the qualification – and optional units where the student can choose which units they would like to take. When the student has accumulated a sufficient number of units they will be awarded the relevant NVQ or SVQ, such as Food and Drink Service – Bar Service or Door Management. Some of the higher level NVQ/SVQs also include mandatory key skills, and some colleges offer value-added modules which can be taken along side the NVQ/SVQ to enhance the whole learning process.

From this point on in this chapter NVQs and SVQs will be referred to as NVQs unless there is a difference in practice between the two.

NVQs are awarded via three main lead bodies: City and Guilds; Training and Enterprise Companies, Local Enterprise Companies, and Training and Employment Agencies; and the Hospitality Training Foundation.

City and Guilds (C&G) . . .

Normally this awarding body does not have a fixed pre-entry qualification for levels 1 and 2, although some colleges may set some pre-entry tests, usually in the areas of English and mathematics. For level 3 and above, acquisition of the previous level or equivalent prior learning is usually required. These qualifications can be obtained on a full-time, part-time or day-release basis. C&G is the lead body used by most colleges of further education. C&G also accredit a series of international awards for overseas students, which run in parallel to NVQ qualifications – International Vocational Qualifications (IVQs). For further information contact City and Guilds at 1 Giltspur Street, London EC1A 9DD. Tel: +44 (0) 20 7294 2468. Fax: +44 (0) 20 7294 2400. Web site: http//www.city-and-guilds.co.uk

Training and Enterprise Companies (TECs), Local Enterprise Companies (LECs) and Training & Employment Agencies (T&EAs) . . .

TECs were a government initiative set up in 1990/1. There were 81 TECs set up in England and Wales each dealing with a given territory, and 22 LECs in Scotland that fulfilled the same role as the TECs. T&EAs are the equivalent body in Northern Ireland. Their purpose is to help local people and local businesses by maximizing their human resource potential in business, enterprise and the local labour market. As a consequence much of their work is done in partnership with local key agencies, i.e., colleges and employers. Due to recent rationalization the number of TECs, LECs and T&EAs has now been reduced, and the emphasis has shifted to training for the needs of the local community, especially for smaller businesses.

By investing in people and businesses they are able to support the Modern Apprenticeship and National Training Certificate schemes, promote good practice in business, assist businesses with training and development, act as adviser and provide training. This unique service aids those who are unemployed and actively seeking employment, people with disabilities and school leavers or adults seeking retraining.

For further information contact the local TEC, LEC or T&EA.

Hospitality Training Foundation (HTF) . . .

The Hospitality Training Foundation was previously known as the Hotel and Training Foundation or the Hotel and Catering Training Company. The change in name more accurately reflects the current activities undertaken by the foundation. The HTF's main role is to improve information about the whole of the hospitality industry and work towards developing qualifications. These activities are supported by three training divisions: The

Stonebow Group, the Hospitality Awarding Body and the Hotel and Catering Training Company. As a commercial venture they provide support and training materials, mainly to the hotel and catering sectors of the hospitality industry. The Stonebow Group concentrates on offering short courses, training and consultancy services to companies intending to introduce training. The Hospitality Awarding Body awards NVQs to trainees. The Hotel and Catering Training Company provides youth and adult training programmes, Modern Apprenticeships and National Training Certificates.

For further information apply to the Hospitality Training Foundation, 3rd Floor, International House, 7 High Street, London W5 5DB. Tel: 020 8579 2400. Fax: 020 8840 6217. Web site: http//www.htf.org.uk

Modern Apprenticeships (MAp)

Modern Apprenticeships are primarily aimed at school leavers, are vocationally based and are for those who want to gain qualifications while at work, rather than embarking on a course of full-time study. The qualifications being worked towards are NVQ based, and although there is no fixed time frame most people take between 2 and 3 years to acquire the required number of units to gain full accreditation of the appropriate NVQ. All MAps are awarded at level 3 and above, and include key skills. Those who are successful are also awarded a Certificate of Modern Apprenticeship from the HTF.

For further information about MAps contact the local Job Centre, local TEC, LEC, T&EA or the HTF.

National Training Certificate (NTC)

This is part of the Welfare to Work Programme, recently set up by the government. It is very similar to the MAp scheme, but the qualifications being worked towards are at levels 1 and 2. For further information contact the local Job Centre, local TEC or the HTF.

Business and Technician Education Council (BTEC)

BTEC is an assessment and awarding body for NVQ and GNVQ qualifications accredited by NCVQ within the hospitality industry. GNVQs (General National Vocational Qualifications) are broader based that NVQs. For instance, at level 3 the GNVQ would be in Hospitality and Catering, while an equivalent NVQ could be Food and Drink Service – Bar Service.

BTEC awards NVQs at levels 1–4, in the same way as other lead bodies. However it is probably better known for its awarding of GNVQ's at levels 1 to 3, and for its First Diplomas,

National Diplomas, Higher National Certificates (HNC) and Higher National Diplomas (HND). It is the intention of the government to phase out the First and National Diplomas over a period of time and replace them with the appropriate level of GNVQ. This process has already begun. Some subject areas have changed over, some are in transition. Whereas NVQs are primarily work-based qualifications with an element of part-time study, GNVQs are full-time study-based qualifications which may contain some practical work-based modules. GNVQs can lead directly on to higher education.

BTEC and the University of London Examination and Assessment Council have recently combined under the umbrella heading of the Edexcel Foundation. Broadly speaking, BTEC forms the vocational division whilst Edexcel directly administers the nationally set examinations.

The GNVQ and other qualifications administered by BTEC/EDEXCEL are as follows:

1 *GNVQ Foundation*: level 1; no entry criteria.

2 *GNVQ Intermediate – First Diploma*: level 2; no fixed prerequisite entry criteria, but often taken alongside GCSEs.

3 *GNVQ Advanced – National Diploma*: level 3, equates to two A levels; entry prerequisites are:
   (a) four GCSEs at grade A, B or C, or four O levels
   (b) NVQ level 2 qualifications in an appropriate discipline
   (c) GNVQ Intermediate in a related discipline
   (d) BTEC First in a related discipline.

4 *Higher National Certificate (HNC)*: level 3 or 4; as this is normally a part-time mode of study undertaken by mature students, the entry prerequisites are very varied. They range from no formal educational qualifications but senior employment positions, to perhaps a younger person who, having completed a GNVQ Advanced, or National Diploma, chooses to follow a part-time route into higher education rather than a full-time one. Each applicant will be looked at on an individual basis, and enquires should be directed towards the local FE or HE college.

5 *Higher National Diploma (HND)*: level 4; minimum entry prerequisites as follows:
   (a) One A level, plus three GCEs at grade A, B or C (or three O levels), normally in subjects which test English and mathematics/science
   (b) GNVQ Advanced, or National Diploma in a related discipline
   (c) For mature students, entrance via accreditation of prior learning (APL) may be possible.
      Applications would be made via the UCAS system, see 'Degree courses'.

For further information contact BTEC at BTEC, Central House, Upper Woburn Place, London WC1H 0HH, or Edexcel at Edexcel Foundation, Stewart House, 32 Russell Square, London WC1B 5DN. Central Enquiries via Tel: 020 7393 4444 and Fax: 020 7393 4445. Web site: http//www.edexcel.org.uk.

BTEC also runs a work experience scheme, via the Internet with over 8000 places, to match students with prospective employers. Web site: http://www.illumin.co.uk/btec/

Scottish Vocational Education Council (SCOTVEC) • • •

This awarding board is administered in a similar fashion to BTEC, but more emphasis is placed on the individual modular approach. Thus, especially at the lower level, courses may be unique to the individual, although if the individual wants to go on to the higher levels, he or she may have to conform to an orthodox pattern of modules. Obviously H grades would be substituted for A levels in the entrance criteria. For further details contact SCOTVEC at SCOTVEC, Hanover House, 24 Douglas Street, Glasgow, G2 7NQ. Tel: 0141 248 7900. Fax: 0141 242 2244. E-mail: mail@sqa.org.uk. Web site: http//www.sqa.org.uk

Degree courses

Degrees are awarded either by the university or by the Council for National Academic Awards (CNAA). There are both national and local entry requirements for courses, however, the basic minimum qualifications are two A levels plus three GCSEs at grade A, B or C in other subjects. Mathematics or science plus English are usually required, and many places will require a language, especially for international courses. In Scotland the equivalent requirements are three H grades plus two GCSEs at grade A, B or C. GNVQ Advanced at Merit or Distinction level, will replace the requirement for A or H grades.

Application for a university place is through the Universities and Colleges Admissions Service (UCAS), PO Box 67, Cheltenham, Gloucestershire GL52 3LZ. Tel: General Enquiries 01242 222444; Applicant Enquiries 01242 227788. Fax: 01242 544960. Web site: http//www.ucas.ac.uk. Prospectuses can be applied for directly from the relevant institute from libraries, and from some Job Centres.

Postgraduate courses

It should be noted that various universities are now offering postgraduate courses at master and doctorate level. Applications should be made direct to the university.

GCE O Levels, A Levels, CSE or GCSE

The General Certificate of Secondary Education (GCSE) sylla-buses and examinations have now replaced O levels and the CSE in all parts of the UK except Scotland. The new certificates are graded A to G and grades A to C are equivalent to O level grades A to C and CSE grade 1.

As previously mentioned other recognized qualifications can also be gained. Some of the most common qualifications and their lead bodies are given below. Some of the qualifications are undertaken on a full-time or distance learning basis, such as the HCIMA ones. Others, however, are often gained as value added units in addition to the main course of study. For example, a person studying for a GNVQ Advanced in Hospitality and Catering may also take the RIPHH Certificate or the BII's National Licensee's Certificate. This type of qualification, except for the HCIMA ones, may also be taken as short courses, and will in this case often be run by the local college of FE, TEC, LEC or T&EA. For mature people the attainment of these relevant and nationally respected short courses can be useful if seeking to gain a qualification via APL.

As courses are constantly being revised and updated to meet the needs of industry, it is always wise to check with the lead body at the time that the decision is made to embark upon a course of study. As previously stated, it is also always wise to check with other relevant professional bodies to ensure that the course is nationally recognized.

Hotel, Catering and International Management Association (HCIMA)

This is the professional association for managers and inter-national managers within the hospitality industry. It is also an internationally accredited examination and awarding body, offering part-time courses and flexible modes of study for those already working in the industry. Its mission is to identify, promote and maintain the highest professional and ethical standards for management education and training in the inter-national hotel and catering industry.

The HCIMA runs two programmes of study for those already at supervisory or management level:

1 *Professional Certificate*: designed for those working at super-visory level in the hospitality industry, with at least 2 years previous experience.

2 *Professional Diploma*; designed for managers who normally hold a position involving section or departmental responsibilities.

For further details contact the HCIMA at 191 Trinity Road, London SW17 9HN. Tel: +44 (0)208 672 4251. Fax: +44 (0)208 682 1707. E-mail: commdept@hcima.co.uk

British Institute of Innkeeping (BII)

The BII is, like the HCIMA, both a major professional association for members of the licensed trade, and also an accredited awarding and examination body. Since 1996 it has launched two levels of qualifications, equating to NVQ levels 3 and 4, aimed at raising and maintaining the national standards within the trade:

1 *Qualifying Examination*: the first level of examination is designed to enable entrants to the licensed trade to gain the practical and theoretical knowledge required at technician level.

2 *Advanced Qualification*: the second level of examination is designed to provide business and management skills.

These qualifications are made up of a series of stand-alone units, such as Licensed Retail Skills. These units can either be acquired individually or through a course of block study.

Within this series of units are ones relating to liquor licensing law and the social aspects of the licensed trade. These National Licensee's Certificates, administered and awarded by the National Licensee's Certificate Awarding Body (NLCAB), a wholly owned subsidiary of the BII, cover on-licences, off-licences, and part iv licences. The holding of the appropriate certificate is often a prerequisite required by magistrates before a liquor licence will be issued to new applicants or reissued to current licensees. The BII also supervises and awards the Door Supervisors National Certificate.

Various centres have been authorized to run these courses. For further information contact the BII, or the NLCAB at Park House, 24 Park Street, Camberley, Surrey GU15 3PL. Tel: 01276 684449. Fax: 01276 23045. E-mail: office@bii,org. Web site: www.bii.org.uk

Wines and Spirits Education Trust (WSET)

The WSET is the awarding body for an internationally recognized series of examinations in wines, spirits and liqueurs. The entry requirements are that the student must either be working in the industry or be studying for an appropriate qualification with an approved examination body. A prerequisite of the higher courses is the previous attainment of the lower level. All courses have been accredited by NCVQ, and approximate to the following levels:

• WSET Certificate in Wines Spirits and Other Alcoholic Beverages – level 2

- WSET Higher Certificate in Wines and Spirits – level 3

- WSET Diploma in Wines and Spirits – level 4.

For further details contact WSET, Five Kings House, 1 Queen Street Place, London EC4R 1QS. Tel: 0207236 3551. Fax: 020 7329 8712. E-mail: west@wset.co.uk. Web site: http//www.west.co.uk

Royal Institute of Public Health and Hygiene (RIPHH)

Within the licensed trade and hospitality industries health, safety and hygiene are of primary importance. Therefore, many people have RIPHH qualifications. The Royal Institute, which was formed in 1937, sets, controls and moderates examinations in a wide range of health-related topics, including food hygiene and nutrition. All the qualifications have been accredited by NCVQ:

- Primary Certificate

- Certificate in Food hygiene

- Diploma in Food Hygiene, Advanced Level

- Certificate in Nutrition and Health.

Most of its courses can be followed on a part-time basis, or can be taken as a short course, and the Primary Certificate and Certificate in Food Hygiene are often offered as value added units on the appropriate full-time course of study.
   For further information contact RIPHH at RIPHH, 28 Portland Place, London, W1N 4DE. Tel: 020 7580 2731. Fax: 020 7580 6157. E-mail: ceo@riphh.org.uk. Web site: http//www.rospa.co.uk

Investor in People (IiP)

Investors in People is a national quality standard which sets a level of good practice for improving an organization's performance through its people. It is employer led and ISO9000 may well be part of the IiP award. Investors in People UK was established in 1993 with government support to encourage the development of total quality in the industry. It enables the service industries, in particular, to develop and measure the relevant skills and attitudes in their employees – recognition of the very high importance of the individual employee to the overall success of the business. Organizations work with local TECs, LECs and T&EAs to develop themselves and their staff to reach their full potential. Competencies gained in one area of employment under the IiP scheme are transferable to other areas as individuals develop throughout their career. For further details contact Investors in People UK, 7–10 Chandos Street, London W1M 9DE. Tel: 020 7467 1900. Fax: 020 7636 2386. Web site: http//www.iipuk.co.uk

Welcome Host

The Welcome Host scheme originated in Canada (called Super-host) in 1986 and has now developed to become an internationally accepted award. It was designed, like IiP, to develop the social and customer care skills of employees, and particularly to raise awareness of the importance of first impressions, the greeting by the host, and meeting the actual needs of the customer. Like IiP, Welcome Host is considered to be a transferable qualification and, if gained in one area, such as working at a local tourist board, would still be relevant and accepted within the licensed trade industry. The scheme is administered by local tourist boards in association with TECs, LECs and T&EAs, and run at various authorized educational institutions.

For further details contact the local tourist board, TECs, LECs or T&EAs,

Useful addresses: professional bodies

Alcohol Concern
Waterbridge House
32–36 Loman Street
London SE1 0EE

Tel: 020 7928 7377
Fax: 020 7928 4644
E-mail: alcon@popmail,dircon.co.uk
Web site: http//www.alcoholconcern.org.uk

Alcohol in Moderation AIM
PO Box 2282
Bath BA1 2QY

Tel: 01225 4714444
E-mail: Aim.Digest@btinternet.com

Allied Brewery Traders Association
85 Tettenhall Road
Wolverhampton
West Midlands WV3 9NE

Tel: 01902 422303
Fax: 01902 795744
E-mail: info@abta-online.org.uk
Web site: http//www.abta-online.org.uk

Association of Licensed Multiple Retailers
3rd Floor International House
High Street
Ealing
London W5 5DB

Tel: 020 8579 2080
Fax: 0202 8840 6217
E-mail: nickbish@aimr.org.uk
Web site: http//www.aimr.org.uk

Brewers and Licensed Retailers Association
42 Portman Square
London W1H 0BB

Tel: 020 7486 4831
Fax: 020 7935 3991
E-mail: mailbox@bira.co.uk
Web site: http//www.bira.co.uk

British Entertainment and Discotheque Association
5 Waterloo Road
Stockport, Cheshire SK1 3BD

Tel: 0161 429 0012
Fax: 0161 429 7214
E-mail: night@mondpub.demon.co.uk

British Safety Council
70 Chancellors Road
London W6 9RS

Tel: 020 8741 1231
Fax: 020 8741 4555
E-mail: mail@britsafe.org
Web site: http//www.britishsafetycouncil.org

British Soft Drinks Association
20–22 Stukeley Street
London WC2B 5LR

Tel: 020 7430 0356
Fax: 020 7831 6014
E-mail: B.S.D.A.@britishsoftdrinks.com

British Standards Institution
389 Chiswick High Road
London W4 4AL

Tel: 020 8996 9001
Fax: 020 8996 7001
Web site: http//www.bsi.org.uk

Campaign Against Drinking and Driving
39 Heaton Road
Newcastle upon Tyne NE6 1SB

Tel: 0191 265 7147
Fax: 0191 265 9819
E-mail: maria@caddhq.freeserve.co.uk

Campaign for Real Ale – CAMRA
230 Hatfield Road
St Albans
Herefordshire AL1 4LW

Tel: 01727 867201
Fax: 01727 867670
E-mail camra@camra.org.uk
Web site: http//www.camra.org.uk

Chartered Institute of Environmental Health
Chadwick Court
15 Hatfields
London SE1 8DJ

Tel: 020 7928 6006
Fax: 020 7827 5866
E-mail: cieh@dail.pipex.com
Web site: http//www.cieh.org.uk

Chartered Institute of Management Accountants
63 Portland Place
London W1N 4AB

Tel: 020 7637 2311
Fax: 020 7631 5309
E-mail: pr@cima.prg.uk
Web site: http//www.cima.org.uk

Chartered Institute of Marketing
Moor Hall
The Moor
Cookham
Maidenhead
Berkshire SL6 9QH

Tel: 01628 427500
Fax: 01628 427499
E-mail: marketing@com.co.uk

Chartered Institute of Purchasing and Supply
Easton House
Easton on the Hill
Stamford
Lincolnshire PE9 3NZ

Tel: 01780 756777
Fax: 01780 751610
E-mail: info@cips.org
Web site: http//www.cips.org

Federation of Licensed Victuallers Association
128 Bradford Road
Brighouse
West Yorkshire HD6 4AU

Tel: 01484 710534
Fax: 01484 718647
E-mail: admin@fova.fsbusiness.co.uk

Federation of Small Business
2 Catherine Place, Westminster
London SW1E 6HF

Tel: 020 7233 7900
Fax: 020 7233 7899
E-mail: London@fsb.org.uk
Web site: http//www.fsb.org.uk

Health and Safety Executive
Rose Court
2 Southwark Bridge
London SE1 9HS

Tel: 0541 545 500
Fax: 020 7717 6717

HM Customs and Excise
New Kings Beam House
22 Upper Ground
London SE1 9PJ

Tel: 0207620 1313
Web site: http//www.hmce.gov.uk

Institute of Brewing
33 Clarges Street
London W1Y 8EE

Tel: 020 7499 8144
Fax: 020 7499 1156
E-mail: general.enquires@iob.org.uk

Institute of Licensed Trade Stock Auditors
7 Comley Bank Place
Edinburgh EH4 1DT

Tel: 0131 315 2600
Fax: 0131 315 4346
E-mail: iltsuk@aol.com
Web site: http//www.iltsa-uk.freeserve.co.uk

Institute of Management
Management House
Cottingham Road
Corby
Northamptonshire NN17 1TT

Tel: 01536 204 222
Fax: 01536 201 651
E-mail: join.im@imgt.org.uk
Web site: http//www.inst-mgt.org.uk

Institute of Masters of Wine
Five Kings House
1 Queen Street Place
London EC4R 1QS

Tel: 0207236 4427
Fax: 020 7329 0298
E-mail: institute_of_masters_of_wine@compuserve

Institute of Personnel Development
IPD House
35 Camp Road
London SW19 4UX

Tel: 020 8971 9000
Fax: 020 8263 3333
E-mail: ipd@ipd.co.uk
Web site: http//www.ipd.co.uk

International Brewers Guild
8 Ely Place
Holborn
London EC1N 6SD

Tel: 020 7405 4565
Fax: 020 7831 4995
E-mail: brewersguild@compuserve.com

National Association of Licensed House Managers
Transport House
Merchants Quay
Salford M5 2SG

Tel: 0161 848 0909
Fax: 0161 872 6068

Portman Group
2d Wimpole Street
London W1M 7AA

Tel: 020 7499 1010
Fax: 020 7493 1417
Web site: http//www.Portman-group.org.uk

Qualifications and Curriculum Authority
29 Bolton Street
London W1Y 7PD

Tel: 020 7509 5555
Fax: 020 7509 6666

Scottish Licensed Trade Association
10 Walker Street
Edinburgh EH3 7LA

Tel: 0131 225 5169
Fax: 0131 220 4057

Scottish Qualifications Authority
Hanover House
24 Douglas Street
Glasgow G2 7NQ

Tel: 0141 248 7900
Fax: 0141 242 2244
E-mail: mail@sqa.org.uk
Web site: http//www.sqa.org.uk

United Kingdom Bartenders Guild
Rosebank
Blackness
Scotland EH49 7NL

Tel: 01506 834448
Fax: 01506 834373
E-mail: ukbgjim@aol.com

United Kingdom Vineyards Association
Church Road
Bruisyard
Saxmundham
Suffolk IP17 2EF

Tel: 01728 638 080
Fax: 01728 638 442

Wine and Spirit Association of Great Britain and Northern Ireland
Five Kings House
1 Queen Street Place
London EC4R 1XX

Tel: 020 7248 5377
Fax: 020 7489 0322
E-mail: wsa@wsa.org.uk
Web site: http//www.wsa.org.uk

Useful addresses: licensed trade organizations

Allied Domecq Retailing
24 Portland Place
London W1N 4BB

Tel: 020 7323 9000
Fax: 020 7323 1742

Avebury Taverns Ltd
Sterling House
20 Station Road
Gerrards Cross
Buckinghamshire SL9 8EL

Tel: 01753 482 600
Fax: 01753 482601

Bass Leisure Retail
20 North Audley Street
London W1Y 1WE

Tel: 020 7409 1919
Fax: 020 7409 8503
Web site: http//www.bass.com

Burtonwood Brewery Plc
Bold Lane
Burtonwood Village
Warrington WA5 4PJ

Tel: 01925 22131
Fax: 01925 229033

Century Inns Plc
Belasis Business Centre
Coxwold Way
Billingham
Cleveland TS23 4EA

Tel: 016 4234 3426

Daniel Thwaites Plc
PO Box 50
Star Brewery
Blackburn
Lancashire BB1 5BU

Tel: 01254 54431
Fax: 01254 681439

Enterprise Inns Plc
Friars Gate
Stratford Road
Solihull
West Midlands B90 4BN

Tel: 0121 733 7700
Fax: 0121 733 6447
Web site: http//www.enterpriseinns.plc.uk

Frederic Robinson Ltd
Unicorn Brewery
Stockport
Cheshire SK1 1JJ

Tel: 0161 480 6571
Fax: 0161 476 6011
E-mail: brewery@frederic-robinson.co.uk

Green King Plc
Westgate Brewery
Bury St Edmunds IP33 1QT

Tel: 01284 763222
Fax: 01284 714487
E-mail: Greeneking.co.uk

Inn Business Group Plc
The Firs
Whitchurch
Aylesbury
Buckinghamshire HP22 4TH

Tel: 0129 664 0000
Fax: 0129 664 0073

J. D. Wetherspoon Plc
PO Box 616
Watford
London WD1 1YN

Tel: 0192 347 7777

Mansfield Brewery Plc
Littleworth
Mansfield
Nottinghamshire NG18 1AB

Tel: 01623 625691
Fax: 01623 658620

Marston's Thompson and Evershed
The Brewery
PO Box 26
Shobnail Road
Burton upon Trent
Staffordshire DE14 2BW

Tel: 01283 531131
Fax: 01283 510378

Moreland Plc
The Brewery
Ock Street
Abingdon
Oxfordshire OX15 5BZ

Tel: 01235 553377
Fax: 01235 540508
Web site: http//www.morland.co.uk

Nomura International Plc
Nomura House
1 St Martin-Le-Grand
London EC1A 4NP

Tel: 020 7521 2000
Fax: 020 7521 3565
Web site: http//www.nomura.com

Pubmaster Group Ltd
Greenbank
Hartlepool
Cleveland TS24 7QS

Tel: 01429 266699
Fax: 01429 278457
Web site: http//www.pubmaster.co.uk

Punch Taverns Ltd
Trent House
Fradley Park
Litchfield
Staffordshire S13 8RZ

Tel: 01543 444100
Fax: 01543 443502

S. A. Brain and Co Ltd
Maes-y-Coed Road
Cardiff CF14 4UW

Tel: 02920 414560
Fax: 02920 414561
Web site: http//www.sabrain.co.uk

Scottish and Newcastle Plc
50 East Fettes Avenue
Edinburgh EH4 1RR

Tel: 0131 528 2000
Fax: 0131 557 6523
Web site: http//www.snretail.co.uk

Shepherd and Neame Ltd
Faversham Brewery
17 Court Street
Kent ME13 7AX

Tel: 01795 532206
Fax: 01795 538907

The Pub Estate Company Ltd
26 Ribblesdale Place
Preston
Lancashire PR1 3NA

Tel: 0125 723 8800
Fax: 0125 723 8801

Ushers of Trowbridge Plc
Directors House
68 Fore Street
Trowbridge
Wiltshire BA14 8JF

Tel: 01225 763171
Fax: 01225 774289

Whitbread PLC
The Brewery
Chiswell Street
London EC1Y 4SD

Tel: 020 7606 4455
Fax: 020 7615 1000
Web site: http//www.whitbread.co.uk

Wolverhampton and Dudley Breweries Plc
Park Brewery
PO Box 26
Bath Road
Wolverhampton WV1 4NY

Tel: 01902 711811
Fax: 01902 329464

Useful Websites

Barzone – fun, games and careers for those in the know:
http//www.barzone.com

BreWorld – Europe's largest Internet site dedicated to brewing:
http//www.breworld.com

CGA Datavault – marketing information for the drinks industry:
http//www.cga-datavault.co.uk

Michael Jackson (the Beerhunter) – information and tasting
notes on beers from around the world:
http//www.beerhunter.com

Mintel
http//www.mintel.co.uk

The Licensee – drinks and catering journal:
http//www.licensee.co.uk

Abbreviations used

A level	Advanced level (GCE)
APL	accreditation of prior learning
BII	British Institute of Innkeepers
BTEC	Business and Technician Education Council
C&G	City and Guilds
CNAA	Council for National Academic Awards
CSE	Certificate of Secondary Education
FE	Further Education
GCE	General Certificate of Education
GCSE	General Certificate of Secondary Education

GNVQ	General National Vocational Qualification
HCIMA	Hotel, Catering and International Management Association
HNC	Higher National Certificate
HE	Higher Education
HND	Higher National Diploma
HTF	Hospitality Training Foundation
IHE	Institute of Higher Education
IiP	Investors in People
IVQ	International Vocational Qualifications
LEC	Local Enterprise Company
MAp	Modern Apprenticeship
NC	National Certificate
NLCAB	National Licensee's Certificate Awarding Body
T&EA	Training and Enterprise Agency

Index

OXFORD
UNIVERSITY PRESS

OXFORD
UNIVERSITY PRESS

YMCA Library Building, Jai Singh Road, New Delhi 110001

Oxford University Press is a department of the University of Oxford.
It furthers the University's objective of excellence in research, scholarship,
and education by publishing worldwide in

Oxford   New York
Auckland   Cape Town   Dar es Salaam   Hong Kong   Karachi
Kuala Lumpur   Madrid   Melbourne   Mexico City   Nairobi
New Delhi   Shanghai   Taipei   Toronto

With offices in
Argentina   Austria   Brazil   Chile   Czech Republic   France   Greece
Guatemala   Hungary   Italy   Japan   Poland   Portugal   Singapore
South Korea   Switzerland   Thailand   Turkey   Ukraine   Vietnam

Oxford is a registered trade mark of Oxford University Press
in the UK and in certain other countries.

Published in India
by Oxford University Press

ISBN-13: 978-0-19-568677-7
ISBN-10: 0-19-568677-2

Typeset in Times
by The Composers, New Delhi 110 063
Printed in India by Adage Printers (P) Ltd, Noida 201301 U.P.
and published by Oxford University Press
YMCA Library Building, Jai Singh Road, New Delhi 110001